The ENDLESS QUEST

And Other
Heart-to-Heart Talks

J. P. Vaswani

Other Books by J. P. Vaswani

In English:

10 Commandments of A Successful Marriage
108 Pearls of Practical Wisdom
108 Simple Prayers of A Simple Man
108 Thoughts on Success
114 Thoughts on Love
A Little Book of Life
A Simple and Easy Way to God
A Treasure of Quotes
Around The Camp Fire
Be an Achiever
Be In The Driver's Seat
Begin The Day With God
Bhagavad Gita in a Nutshell
Burn Anger Before Anger Burns You
Dada Answers
Daily Inspiration
Daily Inspiration (Booklet)
Destination Happiness
Dewdrops of Love
Does God Have Favourites?
Formula For Prosperity
Friends Forever
Gateways to Heaven
God In Quest of Man
Good Parenting
How to Overcome Depression
I Am A Sindhi
In 2012 All Will Be Well
India Awake
Joy Peace Pills
Kill Fear Before Fear Kills You
Ladder of Abhyasa
Lessons Life Has Taught Me
Life After Death
Management: Moment by Moment
Mantra for the Modern Man
Mantras for Peace of Mind
Many Paths: One Goal
Many Scriptures: One Wisdom
Nearer, My God, To Thee!
New Education Can Make The World New
Peace or Perish
Positive Power of Thanksgiving
Sadhu Vaswani: His Life And Teachings
Saints for You and Me
Saints With A Difference
Secrets of Health and Happiness
Shake Hands With Life
Short Sketches of Saints Known & Unknown
Sketches of Saints Known & Unknown
Spirituality In Daily Life
Stop Complaining: Start Thanking!
Swallow Irritation Before Irritation Swallows You
Teachers Are Sculptors
Ten Companions of God
The Goal of Life and How to Attain it
The Little Book of Freedom From Stress
The Little Book of Prayer
The Little Book of Service
The Little Book of Success
The Little Book of Wisdom
The Little Book of Yoga
The Magic of Forgiveness
The Miracle of Forgiving
The New Age Diet: Vegetarianism For You And Me
The Perfect Relationship: Guru and Disciple
The Seven Commandments of The Bhagavad Gita
The Terror Within
The Way of Abhyasa (How To Meditate)
Thus Have I Been Taught
Tips For Teenagers
What to do When Difficulties Strike
What You Would Like To Know About Hinduism
What You Would Like To Know About Karma
Why Be Sad?
Why Do Good People Suffer?
Women: Where Would The World Be Without You?
You Are Not Alone God Is With You!
You Can Change Your Life

Story Books:

101 Stories For You And Me
100 Stories You Will Never Forget
25 Stories For Children and Also For Teens
Break The Habit
It's All A Matter of Attitude
Snacks For The Soul
More Snacks For The Soul
The Lord Provides
The Heart of a Mother
The Highway to Happiness
The King of Kings
The One Thing Needful
The Patience of Purna
The Power of Good Deeds
The Power of Thought
Trust Me All in All or Not at All
Whom Do You Love The Most
You Can Make A Difference

In Hindi:

Aalwar Santon Ki Mahaan Gaathaayen
Aapke Karm, Aapka Bhaagya Banaate Hai
Aatmik Jalpaan
Aatmik Poshaan
Bhakton Ki Uljhanon Kaa Saral Upaai
Bhale Logon Ke Saath Buraa Kyon?
Brindaavan Kaa Baalak
Dainik Prernaa
Dar Se Mukti Paayen
Ishwar Tujhe Pranaam

Jiski Jholi Mein Hain Pyaar
Krodh Ko Jalaayen Swayam Ko Nahin
Laghu Kathaayein
Mrutyu Hai Dwar... Phir Kyaa?
Nava Pushp (Bhajans In Hindi and Sindhi)
Praarthna Ki Shakti
Pyar Kaa Masihaa
Sadhu Vaswani: Unkaa Jeevan Aur Shikshaayen
Safal Vivah Ke Dus Rahasya
Santon Ki Leela
Shamsheelta Ka Jaadoo
Srimad Bhagvad Gita: Gagar Ma Sagar

In Sindhi:
Burn Anger Before Anger Burns You
Jaade Pireen Kaare Pandh
Munhinjee Dil Ta Lagee Laahootiyun Saan
Why Do Good People Suffer
Vatan Je Varnan De

In Marathi:
Krodhalaa Shaanth Karaa, Krodhane Ghala Ghalnya Purvee (Burn Anger Before Anger Burns You)
Life After Death
Pilgrim of Love
Sind and the Sindhis
Sufi Sant (Sufi Saints of East and West)
What You Would Like To Know About Karma

In Kannada:
101 Stories For You And Me
Burn Anger Before Anger Burns You
Life After Death
Tips for Teenagers
Why do Good People Suffer

In Telugu:
Burn Anger Before Anger Burns You
Life after Death
What You Would Like To Know About Karma

In Arabic:
Daily Appointment With God
Daily Inspiration

In Chinese:
Daily Appointment With God

In Dutch:
Begin The Day With God

In Bahasa:
A Little Book of Success
A Little Book of Wisdom
Burn Anger Before Anger Burns You
Life After Death

In Spanish:
Aprenda A Controlar Su Ira (Burn Anger Before Anger Burns You)
Bocaditos Para el Alma (Snacks For The Soul)
Dios (Daily Meeting With God)
El Bein Quentu Hagas, Regresa (The Good You Do Returns)
Encontro Diario Con Dios (Daily Appontment With God)
Inicia Tu Dia Con Dios (Begin The Day With God)
L'Inspiration Quotidienne (Daily Inspiration)
Mas Bocaditos Para el Alma (More Snacks For The Soul)
Mata Al Miedo Antes De Que El Miedo Te Mate (Kill Fear Before Fear Kills you)
Queme La Ira Antes Que La Ira Lo Queme A Usted (Burn Anger Before Anger Burns You)
Sita Diario Ku Dios (I Luv U, God!)
Todo Es Cuestion De Actitud! (Its All A Matter of Attitude)
Vida Despues De La Muerte (Life After Death)

In Gujarati:
It's All A Matter of Attitude

In Oriya:
Burn Anger Before Anger Burns You
More Snacks For The Soul
Pilgrim of Love
Snacks For The Soul
Why Do Good People Suffer

In Russian:
What Would You Like To Know About Karma

In Tamil:
10 Commandments of a Successful Marriage
Burn Anger Before Anger Burns You
Daily Appointment with God
Its All A Matter of Attitude
Kill Fear Before Fear Kills You
More Snacks For The Soul
Secrets of Health and Happiness
Snacks For The Soul
Why Do Good People Suffer

In Latvian:
The Magic of Forgiveness

Other Publications:

Recipe Books:
90 Vegetarian Sindhi Recipes
Delicious Vegetarian Recipes
Simply Vegetarian

Books on Dada J. P. Vaswani:
A Pilgrim of Love
Dada J.P. Vaswani: His Life and Teachings
Dada J.P. Vaswani's Historic Visit to Sind
Dost Thou Keep Memory?
How To Embrace Pain
Living Legend
Moments with the Master

STERLING PAPERBACKS
An imprint of
Sterling Publishers (P) Ltd.
Regd. Office: A-59, Okhla Industrial Area, Phase-II,
New Delhi-110020. CIN: U22110PB1964PTC002569
Tel: 26387070, 26386209; Fax: 91-11-26383788
E-mail: mail@sterlingpublishers.com
www.sterlingpublishers.com

The Endless Quest and other Heart to Heart Talks
© 2014, J. P. Vaswani
ISBN 978 81 207 8958 6

All rights are reserved.
No part of this publication may be reproduced, stored in a retrieval system or transmitted, in any form or by any means, mechanical, photocopying, recording or otherwise, without prior written permission of the author.

DADA VASWANI BOOKS
Visit us online to purchase books on self improvement, spiritual advancement, meditation and philosophy. Plus audio cassettes, CDs, DVDs, monthly journals and books in Hindi.
www.dadavaswanisbooks.org

Printed in India
Printed and Published by Sterling Publishers Pvt. Ltd., New Delhi-110 020.

Contents

Do We Need God?-1	8
Do We Need God?-2	16
Sri Krishna: Perfection Incarnate	24
Make The Most of Your Spiritual Energy!	32
How To Conserve Your Spiritual Energy	41
Discover Yourself!	50
Who Am I?	59
That Art Thou!	68
In Quest of the Self	77
The Wonder That Is The Soul	86
The Gift of Sorrow	94
WhateverHappens, Happens for the Best	102
Detachment is the Way	111
The Endless Quest	121
The Inner Light	130

We lay our trust on banks which fail, on bonds whose values fluctuate, on friends who betray us, on earthly power and dominion, on worldly goods that are perishable. When will we lay our trust in God?

Do We Need God?-1

The best beloved Poet-Saint of Sind, Shah Abdul Latif, has the following words in one of his moving songs:

> Thou art the Friend, the Healer Thou,
> For every suffering, the remedy...

Is this not true, that in every suffering, it is God who abides with us?

Therefore, let us call out to Him in times of distress: He is the friend who will never ever let us down!

> Twameva Mata cha Pita Twameva,
> Twameva Bandhu cha Sakha Twameva,
> Twameva Vidya Dravinam Twameva
> Twameva Sarvam Mama Dev Deva!

> Thou art my father and mother, Thou my relative and friend,
> Thou art my wisdom and wealth, Thou art my all!

The saints spoke nothing but the truth. They conveyed the most profound lessons of life in an utterly simple and direct language. God is our friend. He is the helper of the helpless. Trust him!

Talking of friendship, one remembers the great Greek teacher, Aristotle. He provides us with one of the finest discussions of friendship in ancient literature. He distinguishes between what he believes to be genuine friendship and contrasts it with two other forms: one based on mutual usefulness, the other on pleasure. He warns us that utilitarian and pleasure-seeking friendship can only last as long as the utility and pleasure elements are available to us.

Utility, he points out, is an impermanent thing: it changes according to circumstances. So with the disappearance of the ground for friendship, the friendship also breaks up, because that was what kept it alive.

Friendship between the young is grounded on pleasure, because the lives of the young are regulated by their feelings, and their chief interest is in their own pleasure and the opportunity of the moment. As they grow older, and their tastes change, friendship also loses its pleasure. Thus the arrival of a new girl friend often results in a young man snapping off ties with his cronies!

But genuine friendship transcends these changes. To quote Aristotle: "It is those who desire the good of their friends for the friends' sake that are most truly friends, because each loves the other for what he is, and not for any incidental quality." And, Aristotle adds, "Goodness is an enduring quality."

Let me hasten to add, such friendship is not without its pleasures and joys: nor is it without benefits to the parties involved. But it does not seek such benefits or pleasures for their own sake.

How many of us can boast of such friends?

A friend said to me in jest: "Some people come into your life for a season, and some for a reason. It is up to us to distinguish between the two."

There are all kinds of friends. Perhaps, we need them all. We need confidants – people whom we can trust with our secrets, our deeply felt emotions and needs: but we cannot make every friend our confidant! Then there are comrades – people whose companionship we enjoy: people who share some of our interests: people who are fun to be with. And then there are fair weather friends – people who will be with us only as long as they are having a good time with us: or as long as they can get something done through us: people who will 'use' us and move on.

Do you remember your school days, when most of you would have been asked to write essays on topics that are a perennial favourite with most English teachers: "My Best Friend" or "A Friend in Need is a Friend Indeed"? How many of our friends have always been there for us when we needed them?

A true friend is one who is with you in rough weather and tough times: he is the one you can always rely on to help you out of difficulties. He is not just there to share the good times with you; he is ever ready to support you in your hour of crisis, ever ready to sacrifice his personal benefits for your sake, when the circumstances require it.

Let me narrate to you the story of two such friends, Damon and Phyntias. They lived on the island of Sicily, outside the ancient city of Syracuse. The ruler of Syracuse in those days was one of the most cruel tyrants known in history, King Dionysius. He was intolerant, unjust and brooked no opposition from anyone. His people suffered under the yoke of his tyranny. But no one could stop the cruelties he perpetrated against them.

Phyntias spoke out against the atrocities of the king: tragically, Dionysius heard of his outburst, and the worst came to pass. He ordered Phyntias to be arrested and pronounced the death sentence on him.

Phyntias was a young man of truth and integrity. The prospect of death did not worry him. But he wanted to return to his native village and bid goodbye to his old mother; he also wanted to ensure that she would be well cared for after his death. He therefore requested the permission of the king to grant him a respite of a few days so that he could make his last visit to her.

The tyrant King laughed outright. "Don't speak to me of a brief respite," he said to Phyntias mockingly. "I know what you would do if I granted you that respite. You would go into hiding and not return to face your execution. No! You will stay in prison until the day of your execution."

At this point, Damon came forward to offer help to his friend. He said to the King, "If you let my friend go and visit his parents, I offer to be lodged in prison in his place, until he returns. I will be your surety against his return."

Dionysius thought for a while. "Your friend is a rogue, and you are a fool," he said to Damon. "Alright. I will let your precious friend go to his village. But he and you had better be warned. If he does not return before the day appointed for his execution, you shall hang in his place!"

Phyntias protested at the very idea. "It is enough that I have become a victim of his cruelty and injustice," he said to Damon. "I will never leave you to suffer for my misdeeds." But Damon convinced him that he should make that final visit to his old parents. "You will return well before the appointed day," he assured Phyntias. "And my dear friend, should you not return in time, believe me, I shall be happy to die in your place."

Phyntias's protests fell on deaf ears. Damon forced his friend to go and see his mother. Accordingly, Phyntias was granted permission to visit his mother for the last time, while Damon took his place in the prison.

Days passed. There was no news of Phyntias. The day of execution arrived, but Phyntias had failed to report to the jailor. The whole of Sicily was buzzing with the news that a prisoner sentenced to death had been sent out on parole and had failed to return: and his friend was being sent to the gallows by the tyrant King.

Under the barbaric King, executions were conducted at the public amphitheatre, as if such a spectacle would be of entertainment value to the public. On the appointed day, the amphitheatre literally overflowed with people: Dionysius was seated on his throne, with his mocking sneer and his cruel eyes. There was no sign of Phyntias. Damon walked up to the gallows, unmoved by his dire fate.

"So this is your friend's final gift to you," mocked the tyrant. "You were a fool to offer to step into his shoes! Look where your precious friendship has brought you, to the foot of the gallows. Don't you regret your hasty decision?"

"I have no regrets whatsoever," Damon replied. "My only fear is that some mishap may have befallen my friend, or else he would surely have been here by now. But I assure you, I am happy to die in his place. I only ask you this: should he happen to return to you after my execution, spare his life. You cannot punish two people for one offence. As you are the King, give me your word of honour before the people."

Dionysius roared out in laughter. "You fool, you fool," he crowed, "Can't you see that your friend has played a dirty trick on you? He will never return to Syracuse as long as he lives. He has made you his scapegoat, and you are pleading for his life. I haven't come across such a pair of friends like you two!"

As the people watched with bated breath, Damon was led to the gallows. The executioner's axe was raised, and ready to fall on his neck, when a disheveled and distraught Phyntias ran into the stadium, crying loudly, "Stop! Stop the execution! My friend must not be killed. I am here to undergo my death sentence."

He rushed to the gallows, and untied the hands of his friend Damon. "Forgive me, forgive me," he begged. "The ship I was sailing in was captured by pirates, who held me prisoner all these days. I managed to escape from their clutches and rushed back here as soon as I could. Dear Damon, walk away from this place, for you are a free man. I embrace my death willingly, nay, joyously, in the happy thought that I have saved you from an unfair death."

"No Phyntias, no," cried Damon. "I am fully prepared to meet my death now. And believe me, I am happy to die in your place. How I wish the pirates had detained you a little longer! I have already obtained your pardon from the King. You must live on, for nothing will make me happier."

And so, before the astonished eyes of the tyrant King, the two friends stood arguing with each other at the foot of the gallows, each one offering to die in the other's place. There was not a dry eye in the crowd, for the people were truly moved by this spectacle of true love, sacrifice and selflessness.

It melted the hard heart of Dionysius, and he forgave both the friends.

Is this not true friendship? But let us admit, such friendship is rare.

I would request you to find a true friend who will abide by you at all times, under all circumstances. In fact, I can willingly lead you to such a one, who will always be by you and with you, at all times. Such a friend can only be God. He is a Helper of the helpless. When other helpers and comforters flee, He is the one who abides. He is by your side when the darkness deepens, when the stormy clouds hover over you. Therefore I appeal to you, forge a firm link of friendship with God. Visualise Him in any form. Converse with Him; connect with Him and make Him your guide, guardian, mentor and everlasting companion.

There was a holy man who constantly urged people to forge a link of love with God. One day, a rich man came to meet him. He said to the man of God, "I respect you for your noble conduct and your humility. But I cannot think highly of your constant advice to us to make friends with God. God is in His Heaven. Of what avail is his friendship here on earth? You must advise the people instead to make friends with their bankers, chartered accountants and lawyers. These people can really help them in their business affairs. Don't you think we have to be practical and realistic?"

He added, "Please do not think I am being harsh on you. I felt I had to give you my point of view. And, to ensure you bear no hard feelings against me, I invite you to come and spend a day with me in my mansion, which is just outside the town. It will be my privilege to have you as a guest."

The holy man smiled and said to him, "I will definitely drop in at your house when I leave this town to continue my *yatra*."

"O, no!" said the rich man. "My house is not what you think it to be – just another residence! It is a veritable marvel of modern architecture. It is designed by a German engineer and built with the best Italian marble that money can buy. Art treasures from across the world are used in my interior decoration. My garden has been landscaped by a French expert, and the lawns have been laid by an Irishman. You need to spend at least twenty-four hours to appreciate all the special and unique features of my mansion." He added with a smile, "You see, I have friends from all over the world, who take a personal interest in everything I do."

The holy man told him, "I will certainly come when I have the time."

The rich man had good intentions, but had a larger-than-life-ego. He repeated, "Every time you say to us, build a relationship with God, talk to God, connect with God. But I don't need to do so. I have everything. If I need anything, my friends and my people are always there to help me. I tell you, I really have no need of God!"

I will tell you more about this man in the pages that follow...

We have tried many things;
when shall we try God?

Do We Need God?-2

I was telling you about the man who said to a saint: "I really have no need of God."

The man of God told him, "In every person's life a time comes when no one but God helps. Hence, I will continue to urge you: stay connected with God. Sometime or the other, this connection with Him will stand you in good stead."

The rich man laughed. "But I tell you, I do not need anything from Him: why should I build any relationship with God?"

After some time a strange thing happened. He came to see the holy man one day: his whole demeanour had changed: he appeared distraught: his eyes were red with weeping.

The holy man asked him, "Brother, why are you crying?"

He replied, "I have only one son. I had sent him abroad to study Engineering. He obtained an M.S. from one of the best American universities and returned to India. He also found a good job as a managing director of an engineering company. At a very young age, he had bagged a high status job. He was also an intelligent, well-mannered and a well-disciplined boy. Now all of a sudden he seems to be losing his mental balance. He has become eccentric and peculiar. For the last month or so, he has been constantly at the wash basin and stands for a long time washing his hands with soap, and keeps the water running. I have consulted many renowned doctors: they have examined him but are unable to treat him. I have had the best Psychiatrists flown in from the U.S. They call it an obsessive compulsive disorder, and say that it will require long term counseling and treatment to get him back to normal. I am at my wits' end, I do not know where to turn! I felt that meeting you would give me some comfort. What can I do? Can you advise me?"

The holy man said to him, "There is One who can help you out."

He asked, "Who is he? Can you give me his contact information? My secretary will get in touch with him right away."

"It is not difficult to get in touch with Him," said the man of God. "He is everywhere. But you must get in touch with Him yourself! He has no secretary, and therefore, there is no point in getting your secretary to call Him! Call upon him personally."

"What do you mean he is everywhere, I have heard of many names of cities and towns, but nowhere have I come across 'everywhere'?" the man said, for he was indeed puzzled.

The man of God told him, "I am referring to the One who is omnipresent. He is everywhere. He is also near you!"

He said, "How can I approach him? I do not know him. Now how do I go to him? I... I don't think I have been in touch with him earlier..."

"It is not too late to do so now," said the holy man gently. "Dear brother, I am referring to God, the Friend of friends. He is a Friend to us all. Call Him. Seek His help. He will never fail you."

Whenever we are in trouble, whenever we are hard pressed, when we are surrounded by adverse circumstances, when we are passing through a dark night when not a single star doth shine, when we suffer from a disease that the doctors declare as incurable, when we face a financial crisis and are on the verge of bankruptcy, when we are involved in problems of personal relationships – what do we do? We call upon friends; we run to our relatives; we turn to our lawyers, doctors, to government and police officers – but we don't go to God.

But there comes a time in every one's life, when one needs His support above all others. When others fail, God who never fails us, becomes the only Source of support. Knock on His door. He will surely help you in your darkest hour of crisis.

If you are like the rich man in the story, you will turn around and ask me: how can we knock on the Lord's door?

One of the reasons why we do not turn to Him spontaneously is because God has not become real to us. To many of us, God is a distant being. He is a far off, shadowy presence, dwelling on a distant star. I ask so many people, "Where dwelleth God?" With an uplifted finger, they point to the heavens above, as though God dwelt way beyond our reach. True, God dwells in the heavens above, but there is not a nook, not a corner on the earth, where he does not dwell.

I recall the words which are attributed to Jesus. These are not found in the Gospels, but in a less well-known eastern account of Jesus. We are told that Jesus said: "God does not dwell in the heavens above; for if so, birds will reach him sooner than man. God does not dwell in the depths of the ocean – if so, the fish would be able to reach him sooner than man. God is within you. The kingdom of God is within you."

There was a man who met me. He said to me, "I do not believe in God. I do not believe in prayers. I have never ever prayed to God even once in all my life."

I asked him, "Are you sure you have never prayed to God even once in all your life?"

He thought for a few moments and said, "Yes, I remember I offered a prayer once."

"And when was that?" I asked him.

"When I was a little boy," he said, "I had lost my way in the forest. I ran here and there, I shouted for help. I was terrified!

Scared and shivering, in that desperate mood, I cried out, 'Oh God, if you really exist, show me the way out of this place. Let me reach home safely.' "

"What happened then?" I urged him.

"Nothing," he said.

"That's not possible," I said gently. "How could nothing have happened? Surely something must have happened, or you wouldn't be here before me. You must have found your way back to the house on that fateful day. God must have heard your prayer, surely."

"No," denied the man vehemently. "Well, yes, I did get home safely, but it had nothing to do with God! He did not come to my help. I was so scared I sat down under a tree and just cried. God did not hear me, I tell you! But a woodcutter came along. He happened to be passing by, and he told me he felt an urge to pass through that part of the forest. So there he was. He took my hand and let me out of the forest. It was only a woodcutter, who saved me. Not God!"

"Only a woodcutter!" I exclaimed. "What do you expect God to look like? Did you expect a man in white flowing garments with a long beard? Did you not realise that he heard your prayer and came to your rescue in the form of a woodcutter?

A holy man of God was being shown around a new and impressive hospital complex, which had just been completed. It was fitted with the latest and most sophisticated equipment. No efforts had been spared to offer patients the best care possible.

The holy man was shown a button placed by the bedside of each patient. "This is indeed special," the Director of the hospital explained. "In most hospitals, the patient presses a button which rings a bell, to call an attendant or a nurse. But very often, the bell was not heard. Or, if it was, sometimes the staff were confused by various bells, and some patients were not attended to. But now, at the touch of even the weakest patient, this button makes four lights flash – one at the nursing station, one above his bed, one in the corridor and one in the ward sister's room. The lights can be turned off only when the call has been answered, and the patient has been visited!"

The holy man smiled. "Human ingenuity has indeed devised a wonderful scheme to help those in need," he remarked. "How much more wonderful must God's scheme be! Surely He hears the cries of His weakest children! When the weakest hand touches the button of prayer, there is no power on earth which can hinder the signal, or bar the answer!"

It was Tennyson who said: "Closer is He to us than breathing, nearer than hands and feet." What a tremendous blessing this is, that God is so close to us, and that He is always available to us! We can go to Him at any time of the day or night, without previously having to fix an appointment with Him. And we can share with Him the deepest, innermost secrets of our hearts, without any hesitation or reservation. Others may laugh at us, belittle our fears and worries, call us childish or foolish. But we can be sure that God will understand us. For He loves us much more than we can ever imagine. His love is understanding; it is patient; it is forgiving. We can go to Him anytime we like – but we go everywhere else except to Him!

You must believe firstly, that God is all around you. You do not have to go to a particular place to meet Him. It is always good to go to temples, mosques and churches. But it is not only in these shrines that you can contact God. He is right in front of you, wherever you may be. All you have to do is to close your eyes, shut out the world, open your heart and call him with deep love and longing – and there He is with you!

We need to know God. We need to move close to him. We need to make God real in our daily lives!

But let me say to you, don't wait till you are desperate and drowning neck deep in crisis! Knock at His door when you are happy, prosperous and contented. Forge your link of love with

Him when times are good. Build your relationship with God while the sun shines on you. You don't need a special appointment to meet Him! Begin with a thought of love, a thought of gratitude for all the good things in your life. Begin with His Name on your lips: start with a simple incantation or a prayer or a holy verse from the scriptures: or recite a *mantra* which brings you peace: or a verse of the famous hymn, *Thou who failest not, abide with me!* You can choose a line from inspirational poetry as that of Shah Abdul Latif, *"In my darkest hour, Lord! You are my support, my stay, my all!"* Or a line from the Sikh Scripture: *"How can one who is under Your protection be struck with sorrow?"*

God does not care for the form, the shape, the vocabulary of our prayer. It is the feeling that counts.

You don't have to be learned or highly educated to be able to pray. Indeed, too much learning or education, far from being a help, becomes a hindrance in the way of prayer. Sri Ramakrishna was illiterate; he could not sign his name. Yet he prayed, for hours together. He prayed as one who stood in the presence of God, speaking to Him as a child would speak to its mother.

"Have you seen God?" he was asked.

"Yes," he answered. "More clearly than I see you!"

Truly has it been said, that God who made the world has no trouble being seen and heard by those who honestly want to know Him.

Art is not needed; music is not needed; scriptural lore is not needed; rituals are not needed; ceremonies are not needed. What is needed is a heart contrite and lowly, pure and holy – a loving heart eager to wait upon God.

Prayer is waiting upon God in love and longing. Without this, repetition of set prayers will not take us far. So often, prayers are read from books; they are good in as much as they draw our attention to God. But this is only the first step.

Once you have built the link through recitation or incantation of a holy *mantra*, it is easy to approach God for help. It is like going across to your best friend and unburdening yourself. Once the problem is shared, nature will provide the solution. It is as simple as 'Ask and you shall be given'. The solution to your problems already exists in the universe. It will manifest itself when you seek God's help.

God is omnipresent and omnipotent! He weaves through every breeze: He wakes in every leaf: He smiles in every flower. He has no contact address, for He is everywhere and in everything! For the lay man, such conceptualization is difficult. Hence, God who is formless assumes many forms and His energy becomes manifest in different deities, gods and goddesses, whom you can make your *ishta devata*!

You would indeed be fortunate and truly blessed if you could find a true Guru: for that is the best way to link with God – through a realised soul, who has already formed a lasting link with Him! May God lead you to such an evolved soul!

The love of God is brighter than the sun, cooler than the moon and sweeter and more fragrant by far than honey and musk.

Sri Krishna: Perfection Incarnate

He came here upon this earth long ago! Traditions tell us that Sri Krishna came here 5000 years ago. He came with bewitching beauty.

Born on a dark and rainy night when His parents were incarcerated in the dungeon of a tyrant. He had two mothers who doted upon Him – Devaki who gave birth to Him, and Yashoda who had the privilege of bringing Him up. Soon after His birth, His father, Vasudeva, carried the newborn infant and crossed the River Yamuna in spate, to reach the other shore and leave Him at Nand Gaon, where He grew up as the son of Nanda Gopa and Yashoda. Gokul, the land of the cows, was indeed blessed by His arrival! He grew up in the salubrious environs of Brindaban, on the banks of the blessed Yamuna river. Out in the open He lived; He felt close to nature; He tended the cows, and consorted with simple and innocent *gwalas* of Govardhan. He was *natkat kanha*, naughty Krishna; He stole butter and curds from the *Gopis*, and stole their hearts and souls along with the milk products!

Who was He? Nameless – for a thousand names are not enough to name Him aright. Who was He? The purest of the pure was He, spotless, stainless; in Him was the light that casts no shadow. Who was He? The *gopas* and the *gopis*, the simple cowherds and milkmaids who had the good fortune to have Him grow up amidst them, whose rare privilege and blessing it was to have beheld His beautiful face, with whom He played games and indulged in a thousand divine *leelas* – the *gopas* and *gopis* exclaimed when they saw Him face to face: "We have seen the light of love in His face! We have seen the rapture of love! We have seen the ecstasy of love! We have seen the face of *ananda* – the bliss that no ending knows!"

He came with the matchless music of His magical flute. And, even as He played upon the flute, so our *puranas* tell us, even as He played upon the flute, the very winds thrilled, the trees swayed, the rivers resonated, the buzzing bees and the cooing *koel* stopped to listen, and the stars and moon stood still, and hearts were hushed – as divine melody poured forth from the flute!

Who was He? The light of God shone in His eyes, the smile of divinity was on His lips, the wonder of the infinite was in His gaze, and the fragrance of heaven was in His wondrous words.

He listened to the mystic voice of nature – and He heard too, the voice of the inner realm of the spirit. In due course this cowherd, this mystic flute player, became the greatest teacher of men, the Master of spiritual wisdom. And those who heard Him speak, exclaimed: "Never has man spoken as He!"

Who was Krishna? What was He really like?

Scholars tell us that in His *avatar* as Rama, the Lord subjected Himself to all the joys, sorrows, sufferings and restricting circumstances that ordinary mortals like us are forced to endure, birth after birth. He had His share of triumphs, for He was the dearly beloved son of a great King; He won the heart of a beautiful princess by a feat of valour; not one, not two, but three mothers loved Him as if He were their own. But He too, became the victim of others' greed and falsehoods and machinations. Wearing the garb of an ascetic He was banished to live in the forest for fourteen long years – and this, on the eve of His coronation as *Yuvaraj*. Having completed thirteen years of His exile, He endured the horror of separation from

His dearly loved wife, who was captured and kidnapped by the demon King Ravana. Valmiki's Ramayana tells us how miserable He became, what bitter agony He endured and how He actually lost all hope of being happy ever again...

Sri Rama was an *avatara* who never once claimed Divinity for Himself, nor acknowledged the same, when others worshipfully referred to His Divine powers.

We can say that Sri Krishna was one who was fully aware of His Divinity from the moment He was born! Are we not told in the Bhagavata Purana that the Divine Babe revealed to His awe-struck parents, His form as Maha Vishnu with four arms bearing His symbols of the sacred Disc, the Conch and fully armed with His Divine weapons, to reassure His parents that He would not allow Himself to be killed by His wicked Uncle Kansa? Did not the newborn infant allow Adisesha to protect Him from rain and thunder and lightning as His father crossed the river in spate and the Yamuna allowed her waters to recede so that father and son could cross over to safety?

A *Harikatha* expert once said to me with a smile: "River Yamuna offered her homage to Maha Vishnu as Sri Krishna and became sanctified forever by His association. But you know, River Godavari was not so kind to Sri Rama. When He came back from His encounter with Maricha and found His dear Sita missing, it was to the River Godavari at Panchavati that He turned, asking her if she had seen Sita come to any harm. Godavari did not utter a word! They say she was afraid of Ravana..."

We refer to Sri Rama as *Maryada Purushottam* – the Ideal Man. May I say to you that Sri Krishna was the Perfect Man?

Lord Krishna symbolises the perfect man! The color of His skin is blue; it is neither white nor brown. It is blue, which is the color of royalty. Lord Krishna is the royal one!

His posture is perfect. Observe the picture of Lord Krishna playing flute, and you will notice that His spine is straight, His hands and His feet are in balance. Physically Lord Krishna is attractive. His smile is beautiful. It speaks of joy within. The smile is enigmatic and it enchants all who behold Him!

The image of Lord Krishna that we all love is as one playing the flute. He has Divine charm as a perfect musician.

A friend once said to me that the Flute is the simplest and oldest musical instrument known to mankind. None of us can fail to be mesmerised by the melody of the flute which the Lord chose as His favourite instrument. It is made of a simple reed or bamboo, as we call it, and every cowherd just made his own, by selecting a suitable reed and punching holes in it; for as you know, the flute has no mechanical parts or special components like strings or chords to make its music. It is the most natural of instruments that produce music!

And Sri Krishna plays His flute in the serene and lovely environs of Nature, in an atmosphere of absolute natural beauty! We see Him pictured close to dales and hills, flowing streams and beautiful flower gardens; or on moonlit nights, which cast a magical spell on earth. And His melody is in tune with Nature; it captures the spirit of Nature as well as the hearts and souls of men and women.

Someone asked me, "Why did Sri Krishna choose the Flute as His favourite instrument?"

Dear friends, He plays the flute because the flute is made of 'reed' – which is symbolic of life. If you see, it has many holes - just as life has many dark empty holes. Lord Krishna teaches us to play the flute of life melodiously because it is these very holes in the flute, which make music! At a deeper and more symbolic level, we can say that in the human personality, as in the flute, there are eight distinct aspects: the five sense organs, the mind, intellect, and ego. If you are able to conquer, nay erase the ego and become like a flute, empty the self of all negativities and ready to be played upon by the Lord, then the Lord will take you up, breathe His life through you, and out of the hollow, openness of your heart, the most captivating melody will emerge to enchant everyone whose lives you touch! Believe me, it is only the empty who will be filled with the Divine Music of the Lord! Those who are loaded, filled with envy, hatred and jealousy are incapable of making this divine music and therefore, useless for the Lord's purpose.

Sri Krishna represents the very perfection of Divine Love. His heart overflows with love for all – the *gopas* and *gopis*, the cows and calves of Gokul, the simple people of Mathura and Dwaraka, and especially Radha! Radha herself is considered as the incarnation of Love and Devotion.

Krishna has a heart of love. Krishna is love. Krishna is a positive, radiant light of love and that is why He could draw *Gopis* of Brindavan to His music. The ecstatic *raas leela* of Sri Krishna with the *gopis* – and with his own sweet Radhika – is evergreen in the consciousness of the *bhaktas* of the Lord. The unconditional love and absolute devotion of the *gopis* have inspired poets and singers for centuries! As for the love of Radha, it is held up to us as the perfect example of what we call *maadhurya bhava* – the mode of devotion in which the *jivatma* looks up to the *paramatma* as the Beloved of the soul!

Krishna's love did not end with the *Gopis* of Brindavan. Krishna's love was for every creature, every tree, every plant, and every stone. That is why, Krishna is always depicted, sitting on a stone, under a tree, by the side of a cow. It shows Krishna's love for all of nature. Krishna is shown as playing the flute on the banks of the river Yamuna. This is again symbolic of greatness. The saints and sages have always dwelt on the banks of rivers. The river is symbolic of the pure spirit of the universe, the ever-flowing energy of the universe!

Lord Krishna was the perfect hero in every sense of the word; He was the champion of the defenseless and the weak. He was ever ready to protect His loved ones from danger. Even as a boy, He took on the demons and evil spirits who came to threaten the simple cowherd folk of Brindavan; He took on the mighty Indra, king of the devas, when he tried to vent his anger on Gokul; He subdued the mighty Kalia who was poisoning the waters of Gokul, sparing his life at the entreaty of his wives. Later on in life, He eliminated Kansa and Shishupala, who troubled His people. When Draupadi's honour and good name was at risk, it was He alone who came to her rescue. He guided and guarded and protected His dear cousins, the Pandavas during their long exile. He went as their emissary to the royal court of Dhritarashtra to try and make peace between the warring clans. When His efforts were repulsed, He accompanied the Pandavas to the battlefield of Kurukshetra. At all times, He was the perfect symbol of valour, courage, and faith, which are the marks of a true hero.

Lord Krishna was the perfect teacher, for He showed the perfect blend of intellect and spirit, philosophy and practical wisdom, action and attitude. It was He who gave us that Bible of Humanity, the Song Celestial, the Bhagavad Gita. The Gita is a song of life. The Gita is a map of life. It is a treasure of wisdom. It is Sri Krishna's gift to all mankind. Little wonder then, that the Gita is revered as a world scripture.

The Gita is not about renunciation and withdrawal, or escape from the problems of life. Its message, as Gurudev Sadhu Vaswani points out, is the message of courage; its call is a call to action: *Uttishta!* Arise! Awake! And rest not till your Duty is accomplished! Swami Vivekananda took this as his clarion call to the youth of India.

The Gita provides a perfect guideline for a happy, well-lived, peaceful, harmonious life. And it has the perfect message for those of us who tend to become defeated or depressed by the vicissitudes of life. For Sri Krishna's message is simple and straight: *Sarva dharman partyajya maam ekam saranam vraja!* Renouncing all rites and writ duties, come unto Me alone for Refuge: and fear not, I shall release you from all bondage to sin and suffering. This is my promise to you."

Can anyone of us ask for more?

Krishna was born at a time when the load of sin was heavy on this earth. The spirit of the earth cried out, "O Lord, I am unable to bear the burden of sin. Please come and free me of this load." It is to redeem the sins of his devotees that Krishna was born. He was the perfect Man! He was the perfect incarnation of perfect love! Radha Rani was in search of that love. Radha was restless seeking Krishna. I wish those of you who are reading this will also kindle the same yearning for Krishna as Radha did, so that you too may experience that wonderful energy called Love!

Krishna was the embodiment of all the nine *Rasas*, which makes man what he is. Krishna is Love, Krishna is *Shakti*, Krishna is *Bhramagyan*, Krishna is a Savior, Krishna is a Redeemer, Krishna is Compassion incarnate, Krishna is pure Joy and Mirth, Krishna is a Destroyer of evil, Krishna is Courage, and Krishna is Pure. Krishna is the Perfect One!

My dear ones, Krishna's one message is: *Aaja Vishram Paa*. Let us accept His unconditional Love and become ever blessed!

Give your best to what you are doing. Let all your energy and attention be focused on the task at hand. When the mind is one pointed it is capable of concentration and is free from tension. Live in the present moment!

Make The Most of Your Spiritual Energy!

Man's way of life in the modern age is often compared to a race – and a rat race, at that! We are not supposed to rush through life, wise men tell us; every moment of life must be LIVED, savoured to the fullest. Living life as a race only leads to stress, and a constant feeling of low energy and exhaustion! I am shocked and saddened to hear people in their thirties and forties exclaiming, "I am exhausted!" And these are not manual workers but sedentary administrators who work at their desks, and on cellphones and laptops! This mental exhaustion is largely due to stress. Somehow modern life and stress seem to go together. The way we live, the way we work, the way we talk, the way we function every day, contribute to the constant building up of stress. People rush about all the time, as though they were carrying the entire burden of the world upon their shoulders. People rush about, accumulating what they think they need - only to realise that they don't need it at all. They resemble squirrels in a cage - running, running all the time - but getting nowhere.

Sometime ago, I was in Mumbai when a man met me and asked me: "What do you think of Mumbai?"

"It is a good place, if only you know how to live in the right way," I said to him.

"I feel Mumbai is awful," he exclaimed. "The very air is full of stress and tension."

I looked upwards for a minute and then said to him: "My brother, it is true the air of Mumbai is full of pollution; but there is no tension or stress in the air. Stress is not in the air but it is in the minds of the people who breathe the air. You can be master of stress or you can let stress master you."

It's not just Mumbai. The world today is full of tension. Wherever I go, I find people are tense and nervous. Stress and tension are more common in their incidence than the common cold.

What is this 'Stress' that we are talking about? It is a much-used, much misused term. An expert on stress-management, Dr. Seyle, tells us: "Stress is the wear and tear on your body caused by life's events." It is the sum total of the body's physical, mental, and chemical reactions to circumstances which cause fear, irritation, worry, anxiety and excitement. The trouble with stress is that it drains us of energy, leaving us exhausted.

Thomas Fuller says that haste and rashness are like storms and tempests which break and wreck people's lives and their businesses. The great athletic trainer, William Muldoon observed: "People don't die of disease; they die of internal combustion." Internal Combustion! As we rush about our life, stress keeps on building in the mind within, until it leads us to a nervous breakdown or a heart attack.

We seem to be in a hurry all the time! It is not only when we are on our feet that we are hurrying; when we are seated, at rest, our minds are rushing somewhere or the other. We may be waiting in an outer office, waiting for an appointment with a doctor, waiting for an interview call - but we are hurrying, rushing in our thoughts. This mental rush, this mental hurry is one of the main causes of tension. Day in and day out we work, we rush through life like automatic machines. In this process, we lose our energy – mental, physical, as well as spiritual.

You may well ask me: work done well energises us; how can we lose energy by doing work?

Today, even the simplest work has become a source of stress; even routine tasks like commuting to work, dropping children at school, paying bills and taxes, shopping for groceries, dealing with clients, entertaining unexpected visitors all of these activities, once considered relaxing, have become stressful now!

Let me explain what I mean; twenty or thirty years ago, fellow commuters on local buses became friends; mothers/grandparents who walked children to school would often take leisurely strolls in the park after seeing the children in school safely; shopping was also a source of catching up with the neighbours, chatting with the friendly neighbourhood grocer and spending a relaxed hour or two. As for unexpected visitors, they were a source of joy and excitement! Now, everything, well, almost everything has become added cause for stress. There are tensions, which go with the kind of lifestyle we have adopted. Work or play, studying or meeting people, earning a livelihood or participating in group activities, nothing is truly enjoyable any more! Teachers say that when routine class tests are announced, students groan! Professionals who have worked hard to reach their high positions, don't enjoy their success; they are just stressed over meeting deadlines and achieving targets.

Gurudev Sadhu Vaswani would often say to us, Work Is Worship! If it is done with devotion and without ego it becomes a form of meditation. Unfortunately, in today's twenty-four by seven world, we have no time, or space, or energy to be ourselves, leave alone to worship or meditate.

May I tell you, I cannot help thinking that this is primarily because we have become obsessed with making money! Our secondary concerns are our social status, our acquisitions and possessions, and what 'others' think about us. Thus we are reduced to what Kabir described as grains caught between the two constantly moving surfaces of the grinding stones, crushed by our own actions and feelings!

Chalti Chakki Dekh Kar, Diya Kabira Roye
Dui Paatan Ke Beech Mein, Sabit Bacha Na Koye

When you live life in a rush, you are like a runaway train, which is moving heedlessly on its tracks. The difference between the runaway train of life and our passenger trains is that the latter knows its destinations, and stops at scheduled stations, whereas most of us simply don't know where we are headed!

"We have to work for a living," people tell me. "We are working to feed and clothe and house our families! We know what we want and our attention is focused on meeting our goals in life. It is not fair to say we are like runaway trains!"

Granted, we have to earn our livelihood; we have to work, in order to live. But we must also be aware that life is larger than livelihood! We work to live; we earn money to live comfortably; we don't live to earn money!

Work is no longer worship, as we were taught in our childhood.

A sister once said to me, "Every time my neighbor's cat gets into my garden, I get irritated." Another lady often says, "The very sight of my sister-in-law irritates me." And there is a brother who says, "The moment I see my subordinates, something gets into me."

What insignificant events cause irritation to us! A cat, a friend, a relative, a colleague - and what not! If we cannot change the people around us, we can at least try to change our reactions to them!

Yet another cause of stress is that we are overwhelmed by the problems we face. I always say that problems are wonderful presents that are thrown at us by Providence - only, we fail to recognise the gift because it comes wrapped up in a soiled package. The word 'problem' is derived from the Latin word *"pro balo"* and means that which is deliberately thrown in our way. It is because we react to problems negatively that we create panic and stress within us.

It has been said that a problem is like a pebble. If you hold it close to your eye, it seems magnified, and it blocks your entire vision. If you hold it at an arm's length, you can see its shape, its colour and its size. If you drop it at your feet, you can effortlessly walk over it!

Another reason why we react negatively to stress situations is mental fatigue and exhaustion. We are often apt to underestimate the demands of intellectual or mental work, as against hard, physical labour. Psychiatrists say that people who work with their brains need more sleep and rest than manual workers. When mental fatigue sets in, we cannot think clearly or react reasonably.

Picture to yourself a man sitting slouched on a sofa. His shoulders are drooping. His head is down, and he is holding his chin in both his hands. His entire body seems to be drooping.

Is not this the condition of many of us at the end of a day's work? What a weary burden we have made of a day - which had been God's brand new gift to us just a few hours ago?

A man went to his Guru, complaining of utter fatigue and exhaustion. "Swamiji, I just cannot cope anymore," he complained. "Please help me!"

The Guru took him to an inner chamber, where there were two clocks on the table. Both were ticking away merrily. One was a freestanding clock; the other was connected to the mains with a power cable.

"This clock will keep going for less than 24 hours," said the Guru, pointing to the first one. After just one day, it will slow down and begin to lose time gradually. I have to come in every morning and wind it up to keep it going, or else it will soon come to a stop."

He pointed to the electric clock. "This one you can see, is connected to a source of high power, and with the energy from that source, it keeps going, on and on. It does not need to be wound up every day. It just goes on, ticking merrily."

The man stared at the two clocks, unable to understand what the Guru was saying.

"You must connect yourself to God - the source of the highest, purest and best energy in the Universe," the Guru explained to him. "Then you will not have to be pushed from outside. No one will have to wind you up, or give you a boost. You will draw all the energy and wisdom of the Universe through your connection with God, and nothing can stop you!"

Constant stress leads to fear, anxiety and worry – and these are joy killers, energy drainers!

What is worry? It is a fixation, an obsession that keeps on striking your mind till you panic and lose your energy. Hence the phrase, 'Frozen With Fear'. Worry is born of fear. Fear is the child of 'mistrust' or lack of faith – lack of faith in one self, lack of faith in others and lack of faith in God. As they say, worry is like a rocking chair; it keeps on moving, without getting you anywhere!

An old story tells us of an angel who met a man carrying a heavy sack on his back.

"What is it that you carry on your back, my friend?" enquired the angel!

"My worries," sighed the man. "Truly, they are a terrible burden."

"Put down the sack," said the angel, "and let me see your worries."

When the sack was opened it was empty!

The man was astonished. He had two great worries: one was about yesterday, which he now saw was past; the other was of tomorrow, which had not yet arrived!

The angel told him, "You have no worries. Throw the sack away."

And so it is that we have the wise saying, "In trouble to be troubled is to have your troubles doubled".

Let us learn to live in the present!

Whenever we are confronted by a problem or a stressful situation, we tend to look all over it, all around it, with all its complexities and demands, all at once. Then we are overwhelmed. We begin to panic. Our hearts beat faster. Our breathing becomes quick and shallow. Our blood pressure rises. We become tense. We feel knots in our stomach. All these are symptoms of acute stress!

They asked a woman saint: "How did you arrive at the lofty heights you have reached? What was the *tapasya* you performed to attain such a state? We always find you smiling and cheerful. Pray, tell us, what is the secret of this happy state!"

The saint replied, "My secret is a very simple one. When I eat, I eat. When I work, I work. When I sleep, I sleep."

The people were puzzled. They said to her, "But that is what we do too! We eat when we eat; we work when we work and we sleep when we sleep."

"No," she said. "When you eat, your mind travels far. You think of so many things that you are not even aware of the food you are eating. You don't enjoy the food. You should taste every morsel, chew it swallow it. Alas, you don't do this! And when you work, you are thinking of a thousand things. You must live in the present!"

Therefore, do only one thing at a time. Doing more than one thing at a time divides your attention, increases your stress. When you are talking to someone, give him your full attention.

It may be just a little matter - but is saves you from considerable stress. Give your best to what you are doing. Let all your energy and attention be focused on the task at hand. When the mind is one pointed it is capable of concentration and is free from tension.

Our lives need to be renewed, if possible, daily - through contact with God. The rain of God's mercy pours every day; and those of us who receive it are washed clean, renewed and re-energised to face the struggle of life, as servants of God. May I suggest you a simple exercise? Every morning, as you awaken, close your eyes and imagine the Life of God coursing through every part of your body filling it through and through. The Life of God is in us already: we have to be conscious of it. Say to yourself: Every moment, the Life of God - call him what Name you will, Krishna, Buddha, Christ, Guru Nanak: they are all so many names of Him who is Nameless – every moment, the Life of God is filling every nerve and cell and fibre of my being!

Joy and peace and harmony are our natural states of being. God has blessed us with abundant spiritual energy to live our lives to the fullest! Let us continue to reflect on making the most of this precious creative energy!

Just as we take care to eat nutritious food, and do exercises like walking, swimming, jogging to keep the body fit and healthy, so too, we need to nourish, strengthen and sustain the good health of the mind. Daily practice of silence and meditation are the most effective techniques for making the mind and the soul healthy, stable and focused.

How To Conserve Your Spiritual Energy

Friends, I am sure you have all heard of biorhythm; this is nothing but the rhythmic, biological cycles which influence our mental, physical and emotional activities. Thus some of us do our best work in the pre-dawn hours, the *brahma muhurat*, as it is called; some of us are like owls: we come alive at night! I know a sister who tells her children: "I am not at my best after 10 pm. Don't bring your problems to me after that!"

We all have our biorhythm, which makes our energy levels fluctuate. When our biorhythm is in tune with the natural rhythm of the planets and the earth, with nature's own rhythmic cycle, we function at our best. Though it is true that every individual has a different biorhythm, life and work demand that we show the same level of energy and efficiency to fulfill all our demands satisfactorily. For example, a home maker and mother cannot tell her family that she will not be able to cook breakfast before 10 am; her family cannot be sent out to work or school hungry! Similarly, a teacher cannot tell his students that he prefers to take his classes at six in the evening!

That is why Gurudev Sadhu Vaswani has said: be in tune with the Rhythm of Nature. Be in tune with the rhythm of life. Today there are workshops and courses taught in almost every city of every country on the science of biorhythm. The point is to be in tune with one's body and not to push it too far. This leads to stress and tension; and let me say to you, worries and stress are not only causes of disease, but they are themselves life-threatening ailments! If we eliminate worry and stress from our life, our life would be full of joy, health, harmony and peace.

Experts tell us that values like beauty, love and creativity, help to make life more meaningful and peaceful for all of us. Alas, our lifestyle today is devoid of the time and space for creativity. Much of our leisure time is spent in uncreative activities. We waste time and energy in partying, socialising, in entertaining, in watching T.V serials or reading meaningless novels.

I believe that most families today 'get together' only before what has been called 'the idiot box'. There is no participation, no intelligent reaction, but only passive absorption which does not engage our creative urges. Suppression of creative urges naturally results in loss of creative energies. Indulgence in mindless acts of pleasure also takes away precious creative energy, which otherwise could be sublimated into constructive, or spiritual pursuits.

"What a piece of work is man!" writes Shakespeare. God has blessed us with this marvellous mechanism that is the human body, and that amazing phenomenon of complicated but natural intelligence that is the human brain. I would not be writing this to you and you would not be able to read this without this amazing instrument of the intellect that God has blessed us with! Each one of us is blessed with countless talents, most of them untapped, unused. Our creativity is always a source of joy. Make a list of the talents you possess and feel grateful for them. You may be a good singer, a painter, a dancer, or just a good conversationist or even a good listener! (That is a rarity indeed!) Feel blessed and thank God for these talents.

We have to be aware that our creative energies are not to be wasted. This awareness will come with the knowledge that we are living most of our lives locked up in the darkness of ignorance. Gurudev Sadhu Vaswani therefore repeated this one vedic mantra: *Tamaso Ma Jyotir Gamaya* - 'O Lord, Lead me out of darkness into light'.

The human body is blessed with ten doors, so say our scriptures. Of these, nine are visible, but the tenth one is kept a secret. It is only when we open the tenth door that we will be able to see the light! When man opens the eyes of his soul, he realises that he is but a traveler visiting this earth; that this world is not his home; his true home is the realm of Krishna. When this realisation dawns, he becomes a *jignasu* – he sets out in quest of God.

Do you wish to be freed from the prison of darkness and ignorance? Do you wish to access the tenth door, to see the truth of life with the eyes of your soul? Then you must learn to conserve your creative and spiritual energies. Creative energies are a blessing. Creative energies are divine and positive. They are sacred. They are not be squandered in pleasure hunting.

During our childhood, especially in the middle class family, our parents teach us the value of thrift. They tell the children: Learn to value money. Do not be extravagant; spend only on essentials; do not indulge in luxury; save for the rainy day. The housewives balance their monthly budget by opting for discounted prices. They economise and save some money for the rainy day.

We learn to save money; but we do not value or conserve creative energy! In order to conserve these precious energies we should adopt a wholesome regime/ schedule. We should learn to channelise those energies in the right direction.

Friends, I implore you - Conserve Your Spiritual Energy. Use them for the right purpose. Don't squander your energy in petty things. The question in your mind at this point is - How can we conserve this spiritual energy? What are the steps to be taken? The answer to these questions is one word – Meditation!

As the saying goes: 'Without peace you cannot meditate', and without meditation you cannot get the secret knowledge.

In order to meditate, the first step is acquire control over your senses.

Meditation is not just a spiritual practice; it is one of the best techniques of relaxation and conquering stress.

There are many aspirants, many anxious seekers, who have the yearning to get the glimpse of the light within. But they continue to remain in darkness, because they are slaves of their senses, and of their desires. Why is this so? Our minds are restless; our frustrations are high. We get irritated and angry without any rhyme or reason.

If we wish to conserve our spiritual energy, we have to get to the root of the disturbances. What disturbs our mind is desire; desire for pleasure; desire for possessions; desire for luxuries; desire to be one up on everyone else! The second step to peace is to conquer desire.

The root of all desire is the ego! It is the ego, which consumes away our energies. It eats into your natural love for God. The way to overcome ego and conserve your spiritual energy is: Reduce your desires!

Simplify your life and create space for better things in life.

"The world is too much with us," wrote the poet Wordsworth. Truer words were never spoken! Caught in the mad rush for possessions, power and material acquisitions, we become prime targets for stress.

Keep it simple! That is the *mantra* which can help you reduce stress and tension. Keep it simple! Possessions and acquisitions may seem marvelous - but after a while, you do not own them - they own you.

One day Gurudev Sadhu Vaswani and I were visiting a village. Suddenly a swarm of locusts flew by and destroyed the entire harvest. Gurudev Sadhu Vaswani looked at the earth and said, "Today, the swarm of locusts have destroyed the crops and ruined the earth; but I am sure by the grace of God the earth will rejuvenate and once again it will be green with the crop."

Friends, desires are like the swarm of locusts; they destroy the 'Field of our being'. We have to be careful and alert, so that desires do not crush our energies and reduce us to zombies.

The third step is: Cultivate detachment! Live and love and do your work to the best of your ability. But be detached from your work and your family!

Do your work sincerely; take care of your family to the best of your ability? But do so with zero expectations. In the Bhagavad Gita Shri Krishna says to Arjuna, " Do your duty; but do not be concerned with the fruits of your duty! *Karam Karo Par Phal Ki Ichaa Mat Rakho*!

Develop the spirit of detachment, non-attachment to work and the results of work. Do not be swayed by success and failure, praise and blame. Do not expect rewards – offer your work to the Lord in the spirit of *yagna* or sacrifice.

True love is not attachment or possessiveness. Attachment of any kind, as the Gita tells us, leads to suffering. *Raga*, or *abhinivesha* (clinging and attachment) as it is called, is an impediment – not only on the path of liberation, but also in the attainment of personal happiness. On the other hand, detachment is one of life's greatest lessons for those who seek the true joy of life. In the words of the inspired poet, "If you love someone very dearly, give him wings: let him fly!"

In Gurudev Sadhu Vaswani's life, as in his teaching, the emphasis was on detachment. "Conquer *trishna*, desire!" was the note he has sounded again and again. And in his daily life, detachment was blended with love and compassion for all – for sinners and criminals, for the "fallen" and forsaken ones, and birds and animals. He could never bear the sight of suffering and pain, it spurred him to action and would not let him rest, until he had done something to alleviate the agony of his fellow-beings.

The final step and the most important is practice of silence.

A king once asked a philosopher, "Who do you think is the happiest being in the world?"

"The happiest of men is he who is closest to God."

"How may we get close to God?" he was asked.

"Through the practice of silence!" was the reply.

Significant are the words of the *Upanishad*: "The mind alone is the cause of man's bondage; the mind is also, the instrument of man's liberation."

It is silence which can still the mind, so that the mind is calm and clear as the surface of the lake on a windless day. In silence, the mind will become a source of indescribable joy and peace - and tension and stress will vanish, as dew before the rising sun.

To sit in silence, you must learn to be still. "The more a man does," says an English mystic, "the more he is and exists. And the more he is and exists, the less of God is and exists within him."

Let me sit in silence, so that the God within me awakens. Let me sit still, as a silent spectator viewing the shifting scenes of a fickle mind. Let me but sit, as I sat long ago, in a theatre, watching a play. The actors appeared on the stage, played their respective roles and disappeared. I kept looking on! So too, let me keep looking at the thoughts that come and go – rushing out of the unknown depths of my mind. They are not mine. I have nothing to do with them. They come: let them come. They will soon pass out, leaving the chamber of my mind calmer, cleaner and brighter.

Sitting in silence, you can pray. You can meditate upon the Lord. You can engage yourself in a loving and intimate conversation with God. God is not from you afar. He is wherever we are. He is here. He is now. Anchor your hopes and aspirations in His safe harbour. Where He is, there is absolute Peace.

You too, can attain to this peace, by the practice of silence.

Select a quiet corner in your house. It can be your bedroom, your drawing room or a corner of your living room. Use this quiet corner for the practice of silence. Select a time; see to it that you are not disturbed by the family members or by household chores. Do remember to switch off your cellphone! Sit in that quiet corner everyday, preferably at the same time, and contemplate on your *Ishta Devta*.

While you make it a habit to practice silence and meditation, you must also exercise moderation in all things. In other words, do not abuse your body by over indulgence in drinks, beverages like tea, coffee or so-called 'hard' drinks. Over eating makes you sleepy and lethargic. At the same time you should not be under nourished, because then your body will be sluggish and you will not be able to concentrate or focus on your spiritual practices. Doctors and nutritionists urge us to fill our stomach only two-thirds for it to function well. Eat *satvik* food; eat light food. Do not make your stomach a graveyard for dead animals; instead make it a shrine. Do not stuff your body with dead energies - do not eat meat. According to our scriptures, the human body is the shrine of the *atman*. Make this shrine beautiful by keeping your body pure and uncontaminated.

May I say to you, to conserve energy is one thing, but to regenerate spiritual energy is another! Hence, sleep less and speak less. The tenth Guru, Guru Gobind Singh, had this message to his disciples - eat less, sleep less, talk less. Gurudev Sadhu Vaswani too was a lover of moderation and silence. He spoke little and meditated more; he was full of radiance. Gurudev Sadhu Vaswani's one message was: Open the window of your heart, that window / door which is a secret one. That is the tenth door I spoke to you of; beyond this door shines the light divine.

Every soul is a spark of the divine and the divine is pure and dazzling light. To have the glimpse of that 'Divine Light' one has to meditate and penetrate within in order to open the secret door. The secret door is cloaked in veils. It is the grace of Guru, which removes these veils. But you have to find a space within for silence, where you can meditate and communicate with the Divine.

My dear ones, I urge you to open that door to the great realm of light. Meditate; go within. The world you behold with your senses is self-consuming, limited and finite; the world beyond the senses is fascinating. I have given you the key to the tenth door. It is now up to you, to channelise your creative energies. Let us wake up, before it is too late. Let us not wait for a mishap or a trauma to lead to a nervous breakdown or spiritual exhaustion. May God so bless you that you move forward, onward, on the path of light and use this key to the tenth door successfully.

SPEND sometime in silence, everyday! Put to yourself the question, again and again — What am I? Whence have I come? Where is my true Homeland? Why am I here? One day, the answer will come to you out of the depths within. And to you will be revealed the Secret of Life. You will see, and you will know!

Discover Yourself!

The Gita tells us in unmistakable terms: You are not the body that you wear; you are the *atman*, the immortal spirit within!

What is this *Atman*?

Gurudev Sadhu Vaswani taught us: "Man is essentially the soul, and spirituality is the foundation of a balanced life."

What is the soul?

Gurudev Sadhu Vaswani has described the *Atman* in one of his prayers. He writes in his simple and beautiful style: the *Atma* is pure. The *Atma* is without sin or sorrow. It does not need food or water to survive. It is eternal. It is the very essence of our being. If you wish to search for this *Atma*, you must search within, search for that divine spark which is in every being!

Several cultures and religions simply do not teach people to focus on the world within them; their emphasis is often on words, rites and rituals; on a form or a Being or Spirit outside; thus the innermost spirit remains out of reach of most people.

The Indian tradition on the other hand, has always placed great value on the inner space that is within all of us: on the state of inner silence and inner stillness. In this state of inner consciousness, we will also discover our own Divinity – that we are not the bodies we wear; we are not the insignificant, pathetic, frail creatures that we take ourselves to be; we will discover that we are the immortal *atman*, the eternal, infinite spirit that is *Sat-chit-ananda* – pure, true, eternal Bliss!

In our constant state of superficial existence, we continue to ignore the world within. In our persistent chase after shadow-shapes and worldly wealth, we lose sight of our inner consciousness. We emphasise speech, action and outward show; we forget that there is a far more valuable aspect to life called reflection, contemplation, introspection. Men and women of speech and action, there are very many; alas, men and women of reflection and contemplation, there are very few.

We are content to live our lives on the surface. Superficiality characterises everything we do. We occupy our minds with what we would like to eat, what we would like to buy, and what we could do to impress our friends and neighbours.

We have no time to think of the world within!

We are willing to spend a third of our life (or more) at work or business, to build our financial resources. We are ready to spare time for our chosen relationships, including friends and family. We are willing to spend time and money to preserve our health and fitness. Enough time is also set aside for entertainment, leisure and relaxation. But when it comes to spiritual well-being, we are at a loss; we ask ourselves – what am I supposed to do for my soul?

I would like to tell you, that you owe it to yourself to unlock the hidden spiritual powers that are within you!

Of the soul, the *atman* within, Sri Krishna says in the Bhagavad Gita:

> Weapons cleave him not, nor fire burneth him. Waters wet him not, nor wind drieth him away...He is eternal and all-pervading. He is unchanging and immovable. He is ancient, the same forever...
>
> [II 23-24]

This great reality is difficult for most people to grasp – for so strong, so powerful, so binding is our attachment to the body!

Ancient Indian wisdom likens the soul to a lamp shining within: it is surrounded by three separate sheathes or layers. The mind is the inner layer, the senses constitute the middle layer, and the flesh is the outermost layer.

The soul is the unchanging spirit that pervades all beings. What we call the body, is but a garment that the soul has worn. In the words of the poet Shelley:

> The One remains: the many change and pass:
> Heaven's Light forever shines: earth's shadows fly:
> Life, like a dome of many-coloured glass,
> Stains the white radiance of Eternity.

As long as we remain unaware of this great truth – that the soul is eternal, and that the body is mortal – we become obsessed with the physical, material, sensual aspects of life.

The more we identify with the body, the more unhappy we become!

It is my view, therefore, that detachment from the physical, and awakening to the spiritual, is the first step to true happiness.

Therefore, our rishis asserted: *Tat twam asi* !

Therefore, Jesus said to the Jews, "Ye are Gods."

"Your substance is that of God Himself," said a great Sufi saint.

"Whoso knows himself, has Light," said Lao Tse.

In this sense, spirituality is the key to unlock true joy and peace, to discover the essential Divinity within each one of us.

The Light of the *atman*, the Light of the self, the light of the spirit – it was around this that our glorious culture was built in ancient India. This culture was known as *atma vidya* – the science of the spirit. For spirituality too, is a science, it concerns the discovery of the One Self in all.

Friends, as I have said time and again, the purpose of our birth is to move ahead in the process of evolution of our being. It is sad that many of us often lose sight of this goal, allured by the temptations of this material world. We get entangled in worldly desires. We become slaves of the senses. We indulge in mindless, soulless, superficial pleasures forgetting our real self.

"Dost thou keep memory?" was Gurudev Sadhu Vaswani's constant reminder to us. Let me share with you this incident from the Master's life, related to this query.

This happened during Gurudev's visit to Europe. One day, he was walking on the streets of London, when he happened to catch sight of a familiar face. It was the son of a family friend from Hyderabad-Sind. The friend, a well to do merchant, had spent a fortune to fulfill his son's wish to go to London for his higher education.

Unfortunately the boy did not 'keep memory'. He forgot all about his roots, his loving family and his dear father who had made so many sacrifices to send him abroad. He fell in love with an English woman. He lost interest in studies and spent more time in the company of the woman he loved. Gradually he took to visiting pubs and indulging in late night drinking parties. He had lost sight of his goal; he had lost all sense of direction and purpose in his life.

This is what material entanglements can do to us, if we fail to keep memory of who we really are, where we come from and what the goal of this human life is! Sadly, the distractions of this world are very many! It is so easy to fall a prey to their attractions and lose our way.

We have taken birth to evolve; but we are so allured by the worldly desires that we forget the real purpose of life. Once we are entangled with the world, pride and ego, desire and ambition, greed and pursuit of power and wealth get priority. Our purpose to seek the soul, the Divine spark within, becomes 'low priority'.

We must seek the truth! We must never ever lose sight of the reality of this existence! We must never ever lose sight of the goal of this human life. All else is illusion; all else is a mirage.

Let me add: seeking the Truth does not mean turning your back on life; it is not renunciation or asceticism; it is not running away from the problems of life. It is the source of courage and inner strength that will enable you to take on life's challenges in the awareness that you are a spark of divinity; that within you is a *shakti* that is of the Infinite! In the process, you do not have to suppress yourself. You must not block your positive energies. Be of this world, be human, live your normal life, but be a seeker of the Truth at all times!

One day Gurudev Sadhu Vaswani was taking a walk in the compound of the Mira School. Pointing to a tree at the corner he said, "Can you see that the sun has cast a shadow in front of the tree? Soon the shadow of the tree will move its direction and will disappear in the night. In the same way worldly luxuries and comforts are shadow shapes, they will disappear in the darkness of Life. We must stop chasing after shadows!"

I am reminded of a story of a small boy who was running round and round in the garden while his mother was trying to catch him. His mother asked him, "Why are you running so fast and where do you think you are going?"

The boy replied innocently, "I am running fast because I want to catch my shadow. But I am not able to catch my shadow. I do not like my shadow running ahead of me. I want to get ahead."

The mother laughed and said, "How can you catch your shadow? The only way to get rid of your shadow is to change the direction. Stop running, turn your face towards the sun and your shadow will disappear behind you."

My dear ones, we should also stop chasing shadows and turn to face the sun of Truth. We should turn back to God. We should seek our true self and not the shadow self. The shadow self is made up of the five elements. And as the Christian funeral service reminds us: "Dust thou art; to dust thou returneth." But the soul within is real; it does not die. It is eternal! The soul is the divine spark within us!

A man may be a sinner, or he may be a sage or a saint. He carries the same divine spark within. When the divine spark is revealed as in a saint, then the Light of Love is kindled and true Love, true unconditional Love flows to all— to the sinner, to the criminal, as well as to the good, to the noble. Then that point of Light becomes a flame and the flame becomes a Lighthouse, showing the way out of darkness for millions of lesser mortals.

The Saints are evolved souls. They are pure and have *samadrishti*. Their love flows out to sinner and the sage, to the criminal and the innocent in equal measure. They do not see our faults; to them we are embodiments of the soul divine. This is the Truth. This is the reality. We are all manifestations of the spark of the Divine. The saints see this spark in the sinner and the sage; in the criminal; the vicious and the vanquished; they do not discriminate on the basis of appearance or status.

I am sure you have all heard of Angulimala. He was a dreaded dacoit. His one overwhelming vicious desire was to rob a thousand people, chop 1000 fingers, and make a garland of them all, to wear around his neck. Angulimala had chopped off 999 fingers. But he had to get one more finger to complete his cherished figure of 1000. He vowed to himself one day, "If I am unable to get one more finger before the sunset, I will chop off my mother's finger!" Can you imagine a man more vicious? Don't you think that such a man can never ever see the Light of Truth?

But then, a miracle happens. On that very day, Angulimala catches sight of someone whom he regards as nothing more than his prized thousandth victim! He sees Gautama Buddha, alone, unarmed, walking in the forest. Angulimala is triumphant and approaches the Buddha with his evil intention. He sees the Buddha face to face; the Buddha sees him; saint that he is, the Master sees the Divine spark in the vicious dacoit. And with his one glance he lights the flame within the criminal! We know the story that follows: Angulimala became a devotee of Gautam Buddha; he became a saint following in the footsteps of his Master.

Let us seek the *Atman*! One can best seek the *Atman* in silence. One can get a glimpse of it in silence — not just in absence of sounds, but in the silence of thoughts, when mind is calm and quiet. There is no need to go to a mountain top; no need to go to the riverbank; there is but one need! The need to go within!

Go to a quiet corner, sit in silence and look within. Ask yourself, "Who am I? Am I this body?" The answer will surely come to you, "No. I am the *Atman*."

Many are afraid of closing their eyes, because they see darkness. This is just the initial stage. Gradually this darkness will throw up sparks of light; gradually the veils will lift. This is a gradual process because the darkness we see is wrapped in veils. It is said there are five veils, which are to be removed in order to have the vision of light. Fortunate is he who has the glimpse of the eternal flame/ light. Then he begins to see radiance in every atom, in every speck of dust, in every leaf, stone, stream, in every star, in the Universe, which is throbbing by His Grace. And this is nothing but the Light Divine!

My dear ones, with self-realisation comes the awareness that you and I are one and the same; the same spark of Divinity is within you and me. To reach that stage, you don't have to learn scriptures, nor read books. In such matters, books are dry knowledge; they lead you nowhere. Books do not liberate, books only bind you to dogmas. Books become a burden on the soul.

If we wish to progress on the path of self-realisation, we have to stop identifying ourselves with the body and become aware of the Divine spark within!

Have you ever wondered why pious Hindus remove their shoes before they enter a temple or a holy place? This is merely symbolic of the idea that we move away from our habitual body-consciousness, which in turn, will help us move closer to God.

We have got to move away from the body, even as we move away from the "shoes" we wear!

Swami Vivekananda was an inspiration, an icon, a role model to the youth of this country. He believed that India's spirituality alone could save our sinking civilisation. He was, himself, a mighty spiritual genius who carried to the modern west the message of India's ancient wisdom – that there can be no true freedom without spirituality and that no man is free until he is master of himself.

I request you to dwell upon this idea: there can be no true freedom without spirituality.

Keep asking yourself — "Who am I?" Answer it yourself: I am a peaceful soul. Sadhu Vaswani, my Beloved Gurudev gave us one *Mantra* — Cultivate the soul!

My dear ones, what is the *Atman*? How may we cultivate the soul?

Let us look at this idea in the pages that follow.

Do not remain under the illusion that you are a body-mind complex. You are much more than that. You are of the spirit. It is this, which you have to realise. To understand this you do not need explanation, you do not need reasoning. You need experience!

Who Am I?

In an earlier discourse, we were pondering on the question: Who am I? What is the *Atman*? How may we cultivate the soul?

Today, I would like to narrate to you the story of a great King who also introspected on this same question: Who am I? In the Third Chapter of the Bhagavad Gita Sri Krishna cites King Janaka as the perfect example of *dhritii* or steadfastness. We are told that he attained perfection through detached action.

What is it about King Janaka that makes him so relevant to us in this search for spirituality?

A beautiful story is given to us in our ancient legends. A great rishi, Yagnavalkya, comes to the palace of Raja Janaka, one of the greatest kings this land has known. Raja Janaka sat on a throne but his heart was the heart of a *fakir*, a saint, a holy man of God. This saintly ruler rejoices to see Rishi Yagnavalkya at his palace. He receives the sage, offers his *pranams*, and begs for a teaching at his holy feet.

Rishi Yagnavalkya begins to question the King. "Tell me, O King," says the rishi, "What is the light whereby a man lives and moves and works and walks and finally to his home returns?"

Raja Janaka replies readily, "O Gurudeva, the light by which all men live and move, the light by which they work and walk and then to their homes return is the light of the Sun!"

Rishi Yagnavalkya smiles. "When the Sun has set, when its light has disappeared, what is the light whereby men live and move and work and walk and then to their homes return?"

The King replies, "When the Sun has set, men must live and move, work and walk and then to their homes return by the light of the moon."

"And what if the sun and the moon have both disappeared?" queries the rishi.

"Then, men must live and move and work and walk by the light of the fire," says the King.

"When the light of the sun, the moon and the fire have all gone out," continues the rishi, "What is the light by which men can live and move and work and walk and to their homes return?"

The King is puzzled. He has no ready answer. He begs the rishi to enlighten him.

Then it is that Rishi Yagnavalkya gives him the teaching – which I believe is the message of Hinduism to modern civilization. The rishi tells the King: "When all external light has gone out – when the sun does not shine, when the moon is not radiant and the fire is put out – there is still one Light that shines. It is the Light of the *atman,* the light of the spirit. It is this, which is the light of all lights. It is by this light that the sun shines, the moon is radiant and the fire is aglow. It is this light by which man must live and work and walk and to his eternal home return."

The Light of the *atman,* the Light of the self, the light of the spirit – it was around this that our glorious culture was built in ancient India. This culture was known as *atmavidya* – the science of the spirit. For, as I said to you, spirituality too, is a science, it concerns the discovery of the oneself in all.

King Janaka was blessed to have Yajnavalkya as one of his teachers. It is said that Yajnavalkya was in Janaka's court until he retired to the *tapobana* (forest of meditation) to take up *sannyasa.*

King Janaka once decided to perform a special *yajna* for the welfare of his subjects. Word went round that the rishis and sages who participated in the *yajna* would be given rich gifts, including one thousand cows.

Now, there was a sage called Udalaka, who was a great scholar and teacher of Vedanta. He had a disciple named Kagola, who was virtuous and devoted but not really astute or learned. Sage Udalaka set greater store by virtue and good conduct, rather than learning; so he gave his daughter Sujata in marriage to Kagola.

Sujata became pregnant, and the child who was conceived in her womb, grew up listening to the vedic recitals in his grandfather's *ashram*. He absorbed the wisdom of the holy scriptures even before birth. But his father, Kagola, often made mistakes in the recital and pronunciation of the scriptures. When the child in the womb heard these, he would twist his body in pain and anguish. Thus it came to pass that he was born with eight crooked bends in his body. This gave him the name of Ashtavakra, which means "Eight crooked bends".

When Sujata heard about the *yajna* that was to be performed at King Janaka's court, she urged her husband Kagola to go to Mithila and participate in the *yajna*, so that he might earn some wealth for the benefit of their son, Ashtavakra. But unfortunately, Kagola was defeated in a debate by Bandi, a reputed scholar at the king's court, and drowned to death as a penalty.

Ashtavakra grew up, taking his grandfather to be his father. He became a great scholar even in his boyhood, and at the young age of twelve he had already completed his study of the Vedas and the Vedanta.

When Ashtavakra learnt that Udalaka was not his father and that his own father Kagola, had lost his life at a debate in King Janaka's court, he decided to confront the king, and seek an explanation from the scholars and sages in his court about the fate of his father.

In the meanwhile, King Janaka had a dream. He dreamt that he was a beggar, destitute and starving. He was in the throes of extreme hunger, indeed acute starvation. He woke up with a start and was profoundly moved by his dream. He asked himself: What is the Truth? Who am I, am I the king who dreamt that he was a beggar, or the beggar who is dreaming that he is a king?

Determined to get to the truth, he summoned all the sages and scholars as was his wont and requested them to give the answer to his question – offering half his kingdom for a satisfactory reply. Many scholars came, for many were tempted by the consideration of the hefty reward offered: no less than half the kingdom. But not a single one of them could provide a suitable answer to the king's question.

Ashtavakra by now arrived in Mithila, accompanied by his uncle Svetaketu. On their way to the palace, they were stopped by the approach of the king and his retinue. The King's soldiers and guards marched ahead of the procession, shouting: "Move away. Make way for the King."

Ashtavakra stood before them and said to them, "O royal attendants, our *shastras* say that even the king, if he is righteous, has to move and make way for the blind, the deformed, the fair sex, and *brahmanas* learned in the Vedas. This is the rule enjoined by the scriptures, and King Janaka surely knows this."

The king, surprised at these wise words of the young brahmin boy, stopped his retinue, and allowed the youngster to move ahead. He said to his attendants: "This boy may be no more than a stripling. But he speaks the truth. Fire is fire whether it is a tiny flame or a huge conflagration."

Ashtavakra and Svetaketu moved on and entered the venue of the king's assembly. Here too, the gatekeeper stopped them and said: "Where do you think you are going? This is a *yajnashala*, and there is no place for boys. The right of entry is reserved for venerable scholars learned in the Vedas."

Ashtavakra replied: "Don't judge us by appearances. We are not mere boys. We have observed the necessary vows and have learnt the Vedas. Those who have mastered the truths of the Vedanta will not judge another on mere considerations of age or appearance."

"Don't give me any more of your cheek," said the gatekeeper. "Just get out of this place."

Ashtavakra replied: "Gatekeeper, grey hair does not prove anything! The ripeness of the soul is not visible only in wrinkles. Kindly inform the King that I am here to meet the court Pandit Bandi."

At that moment the king himself came there and easily recognised Ashtavakra, the precociously wise boy he had met a few minutes earlier. He ordered the gatekeepers to allow the two youngsters to enter the assembly hall.

Many eminent rishis and scholars were seated on their grand and honourable places when Ashtavakra entered the hall. As he hobbled into the hall, moving his crooked figure towards the conclave, the sages who were already seated burst out in derisive laughter.

Ashtavakra paused, and then addressed the king. "I thought I was going to attend a meeting of philosophers," he said to Janaka. "But it would appear that I have walked into a gathering of cobblers!"

"How dare you..." protested one of the scholars, rising to his feet in anger.

Raja Janaka said to the young sage in all humility, "Please explain yourself, wise one."

"The men whom you have gathered here are looking at my flesh, my skin. What can they be but cobblers? This physical body that I wear is but a shoe. These men are judging me by the shoes I wear. They do not realise that I am not this body. How can these men be philosophers?"

The sages and scholars could only bow down their heads in shame!

Ashtavakra then turned to the King. "They tell me that you are going to give away half your kingdom in return for an answer that you seek to your question. But you must tell me how you can do this – does this kingdom belong to you?"

Taken aback, the King replied, "But of course it belongs to me; I have inherited it by due rights by my royal lineage."

"May I ask who owned the kingdom before you came to the throne?"

"My father."

"And before that?"

"My father's father."

"And, after you?"

"My sons will inherit this kingdom, even as I did."

"So you see, mighty king, this kingdom did not belong to you earlier, and it will not be yours in the future. Yet you claim ownership in between, and even assume the right to give a part of it away..."

The king realised that there was a serious flaw in his assumptions, and that he was actually only the caretaker of the kingdom and that it did not belong to him. Ashtavakra had made it clear to him that he could not give away what he did not own.

"Now tell me, what will you give me if I answer your question?"

The King replied in a small voice, "I offer you my body, which is my own."

"Oh King, you are making the same mistake again," laughed Ashtavakra. "Are you sure you are the owner of this body?"

"Yes, of course, I am the dweller in this body, therefore I own it, and everything is under my control."

"May I ask you, where was this body of yours 100 years ago and where will it be 100 years from now?"

Again the king had to concede that the body did not really belong to him either and that it was just given to him on loan by Mother Nature for the duration of a lifetime, after which it would have to be returned to Nature.

"Alright, said the king, "I'll give you my mind."

"You think you own your mind; you cannot even control your mind. How can you give something over which you have no control? You tell your mind to do this and it does not even listen to you?"

Eventually King Janaka realised that he was in the presence of a great Master, and asked to be accepted as Ashtavakra's disciple to be taught the mysteries of the Self.

The essence of the dialogue between King Janaka and Ashtavakra is beautifully rendered in the Ashtavakra Gita.

Many of us are given to making tall claims: "I know this," "I can do this," "I am so and so, such and such is my designation," "I am such a one," I am the doer," "I am the giver," – how vain and futile are such assertions!

> Here is how a great poet saint puts it:
> When my ego was struck by the sword that is the Guru's love,
> That love began to kill my ego.
> Even when I was alive, I experienced death.
> My death died; and I became immortal.

The ego is subtle; its workings are not obvious. As the seeker is making progress on the path, he may pride himself on his efforts. Sometimes he thinks he is close to success. Sometimes he feels he has attained his goal. Sometimes he realises with despair, that it is very difficult to be spiritual.

Then comes to him the realisation that his efforts and endeavours are not pure but tainted, spotted. The darkest spot of them all, he realises, is the ego – the lower self – the 'I'. And then he begins to realise that he must transcend the ego to enter into the Limitless. He begins to realise that of his own accord, he can do nothing, achieve nothing. He learns to accept all that comes to him – abasement, criticism, disappointments – as the Will of God. As the love of God and Guru fills him, egoism dies. When this happens, he is reborn – born again in the life of the spirit.

This, I humbly submit, is the essence of a *dwija* – one who is twice born. He is born once in the flesh; he is reborn when he realises that he is not the body he wears!

This is what happened to King Janaka. He learnt this great truth from one sage; he passed it on to others!

King Janaka also serves to illustrate the point that spiritual awareness is not the exclusive prerogative of a certain 'type' of people – people who are unworldly, committed to self-enforced poverty, prone to asceticism, self-denial or given to renunciation. People in power, people wielding authority, wealthy and influential people can take to spirituality if they so desire. Equally, householders, businessmen, scholars, office workers and students too, can take to spirituality.

Each one of us has the indwelling *atman*; so each of us is eligible to practice spirituality in our daily life. Our awareness is all that it takes to set out on the path!

The human soul is a spark of the Universal Spirit or God as we call Him. When we live our daily life in the realization of this truth, the body becomes a temple that is worthy to be inhabited by the Spirit! Discover God within you.

That Art Thou!

We once asked Gurudev Sadhu Vaswani, "What is the beginning of the spiritual life?"

Gurudev's answer was clear and precise. "When I lose myself, I find the Soul."

Finding your soul – that is the essence of spirituality!

There is something in each one of us beyond the reach of words. It breaks out at times in a simple gaze of the eye, in an understanding smile, in an invisible ray of the heart which travels out to a fellow pilgrim on the path, a kindred soul. If only we could learn to work the inner wireless, there would be no need to speak, perhaps no need to read books!

Don't mistake my words. I love books. We must all continue to read books. But we must not allow books to become a barrier on the way we choose to walk. I am not here to talk to you about the vanity of learning or the display of acquired wisdom. I am only sharing with you the reflections that a pilgrim on the path wishes to share with his fellow seekers. We must all continue to read good books; but we must not stop with reading; we must pause for further reflection: but above all, we must practise more! Let your reading be reflected in deeds of daily life. When you choose to walk the way of the spirit, you must become a ladder unto yourself to reach beyond yourself!

In the simplest terms, spirituality is the aspiration, the genuine effort to know our true self. As I said earlier, it begins with the realisation that we are not the bodies we wear; that this materialistic world we live in, cannot satisfy our deepest aspirations; that our unquenchable desire for wealth and power cannot really give us the joy and peace that we truly crave...

The problem with many of us is that we have completely identified ourselves with the body – the physical, material aspects of our existence. If I were to ask, "Who are you?" you would immediately point to your physical form. If I were to ask you, "Who is J. P.Vaswani?" you would point to my form, my physical body.

But we are not the bodies we wear! This is the first teaching that the Lord gives us in the Gita. The body is only a garment we have worn during this present earth incarnation.

As the soul experienceth, in the body, childhood, youth and age, so passeth on to another body. The *dheera*, the sage, is not perplexed by this. (Ch:II:13 Bhagavad Gita)

When I urge you not to identify yourself with the body, I am asking you to move away from the allurements of the materialistic world. The more we identify with the body, the more we want, the more we crave, the more we desire to possess, the more we get entangled in *maya*.

Once upon a time, there lived a wise and holy sage who had attained spiritual illumination. Many were the people who knocked at his door, eager to see him, speak to him and be blessed by him.

Whenever there was a knock at his door, he would ask "Who are you?" The visitor would invariably say, "I am so-and-so, son of so-and-so, from such-and-such-village."

"Why have you come?" the sage would ask next.

"O holy one, give me your blessings so that..." and the visitors would place their desires before the holy one. "So that I can have a rich harvest...", "So that I may have a son..." and so on.

Receiving such answers, the sage would lapse into silence. He would not open the door. Thus many people came to him and went away disappointed.

One day, a seeker came to knock at the holy man's door.

"Who are you?" called out the sage.

"I wish I knew," came the answer. "Oh holy one, I beg you to enlighten me, for I don't know who I am, and why I came into this world. Please show me the way, so that I may attain the true goal of this, my human life."

The holy man was well pleased with this reply and opened his door to admit the seeker. He realised that the man was a genuine aspirant, thirsting for the Truth. He took him as his disciple, and initiated him on the path of self-realisation.

Ask yourself, "Who am I?" Look for the answer in the heart within. "Where do I come from? Why am I here? What is the purpose of this existence of mine?" You will be led to the truth that you are not the body you wear!

Identification with the body leads to the illusion that power, pleasures and possessions of this world can make us happy. But this is not true; instead, these material possessions only keep us in bondage – the bondage of ignorance, *avidya*. Once you are freed from this illusion, you will realise the truth of the Self, and move towards God-realisation. This is the process by which we may all move from illusion to reality; from darkness to light; from death to immortality.

The soul, the *atman*, the indwelling one, passes from body to body. It is unaffected by outer things. The Self abides; the bodies are transient.

You may well ask: why does the soul pass from body to body? My answer is: to gather experiences, and to evolve towards its abode in the Eternal. Just as the diverse bodies of our childhood, youth and age do not cause a doubt in our minds about the continuity of the self, so too, the diverse bodies of different incarnations, especially the new body after death, should not cause us to doubt the continuity of the *atman*.

The Lord tells Arjuna: you have always been; you will always be. This is the awareness that we must try to attain – that we are immortal, that we abide in Eternity.

You are not the body! You are the immortal soul within! Therefore, do not become a slave of the body. Do not keep running after the shadow shapes that come and go!

St. Francis of Assisi once observed that the root of all evil, the root of all sin, is this sense of identification with the body. You are not this body that you wear – this body is only your present, temporary address. You inhabit the body now. In your earlier incarnation, you lived elsewhere – you were in a different body. Now you live in another – but not for long. Sooner or later, your address will change. You will move on.

The body is the dress you have worn. It is a boat which you are rowing, to cross the *sansar sagar* – the ocean of transmigration. It is meant to take you to the other shore.

There are some people who go one step further. They identify themselves with the body-mind complex.

It is the body-mind complex that is affected by the impressions of sense- life. These impressions are impermanent, transient. Therefore, the Roman thinker Marcus Aurelius said, "Things themselves do not touch the soul. Let that part of thy soul which leads and governs, be untouched by the movements of the flesh, whether of pleasure or of pain."

The mind receives its impressions from the outside world, conveyed to it through the five senses. And the mind swings between joy and sorrow, happiness and dejection, excitement and inertia, elation and defeat.

Have I won the lottery? I am excited. Have I won an award? I am delighted. Have I received a substantial increment in my salary? I am pleased. Has someone praised me? Are good things happening to me? I'm content. I think life is just fine.

But life is not always so pleasant. Sometimes I lose money in business, I am depressed, someone criticises me, I am downcast. My work is not recognised or appreciated, I lose all interest in work. I withdraw. I cut myself off from others. I grow in despondency and despair...

We are not the body, or the mind. What are we then? *Tat Twam Asi* – That art Thou! What That is, we have yet to discover. We have to enter upon a voyage of discovery – not like the voyages taken up by Drake and Magellan who circumnavigated the world – but the voyage of self-discovery.

My friends, I urge you to become aware of the value of this human birth. It is priceless! It has been bestowed upon each one of us for a specific purpose – that we may realise what we are, whence we came, and wither we are to return.

We are not the bodies that we wear. We are immortal spirits. We are not this; we are That!

Every day, as you wake up in the morning, I urge you to repeat this *mahavakya* given to us by the rishis of our ancient land – *Tat Twam Asi!* That Thou art! Thou art not this, the body, that thou take thyself to be. Thou art the immortal soul! This is the very first commandment of the Bhagavad Gita – Thou shalt never, never identify thyself with the body!

The body is *asat*: it is material; it is destructible. But the *atman* is imperishable; of this imperishable soul, the Lord says in the Gita:

> He never is born, nor does he, at any time, die. Nor, having once come to be, does he cease to be. He is unborn, perpetual, eternal, ancient. He is not slain when the body is slain. (Bhagavad Gita Ch. II:20)

Does not this assert the truth – *Tat Twam Asi!*

Tat Twam Asi! That art thou! In the *Mundaka Upanishad*, we are told of two birds perched on the branches of the selfsame tree. One of them is always looking up at the sky; it is ecstatic, energetic and sings a song of divine beauty. The other bird, perched on a lower branch, glances downwards, and is overwhelmed by anguish and misery.

The two birds symbolise the Self – the first, which looks upward, has discovered the essential glory of the Divine Self within. The second is attached to the body, to the earth, and is weighed down by attachment and grief.

Have you read that beautiful part of the *Ramayan*, where Jambhavan awakens Hanuman's spiritual power and reminds him that he is not what he seems – a mere *vanara*? Hanuman is diffident and doubtful at first – he feels that he will never be able to cross the sea and travel to Lanka. But the wise Jambhavan helps him unleash his divine potential.

Each one of us has a Hanuman asleep inside us – a tremendous soul-force that will help us cross the ocean of *maya*. This hidden *shakti* can be awakened by a guru's guidance.

The guru will unfold to our consciousness the truth that inside each one of us is *sat chit ananda* – true, eternal, blissful knowledge. Alas, so busy are we in living the life of the body, that we have forgotten this, our essential nature. The *guru* can awaken us anew to this realisation.

There is a story I read somewhere, according to which Sri Rama once asked Hanuman to explain to him how the two of them were related to each other. Hanuman is said to have replied, "O Lord, from a physical point of view, when I regard myself as the body, I am your slave. From the mental perspective, I am a ray, an emanation, while you are the Sun, the Light everlasting. But from the perspective of the spirit, I am none other than your Self!"

What a wonderful story this is! Insofar as we do have a body, let this body be an instrument, a slave of the Lord. Let us seek union with the Lord through all that we are – in body, in mind and spirit. Let us use the body to perform God's will. Let us use the mind to radiate God's love and wisdom. In the spirit within, let us seek identity with God.

The question that every spiritual aspirant has to ask himself again and again is this: Who am I? Who am I?

For many of us, our life on earth is nothing more than parade of ego-desires. As the ego changes, our desires too change. The little child craves toys; the young boy wants computer games and gadgets; the young man chases after fast cars and girls; the grown-up man chases wealth and power. And so we hanker after shadow shapes, fondly imagining that fulfilling the ego desires will make us happy.

From birth to birth, from one life to another, the ego changes its shape and form like a cloud – the cloud that hides the sun, the source of light, the sense of our real identity.

Identification with the body, egoism and ignorance of the true nature of the self – these three are identified by sages as the cause of all human suffering. Egoism can only be removed by the purification of the mind and the senses – and this is best achieved through selfless, desireless action – *nishkama karma*, as recommended by the Lord in the Gita.

Therefore, have the rishis of ancient India taught us: Assert your essential nature – and be free! Realise the Divine within you – and be free! Expand your consciousness, purify the mind, discover the true self – and you will recollect your essential nature – *soham* – I am That!

Do not be a miser – do not cling to the body, unable to spend your infinite spiritual wealth. Let go of ignorance – let go of the ego – and the humiliating notion that you are limited, restricted by the body and the mind. Realise that you belong to infinity, that your soul is immortal, that God's power and grace sustain you – and that you are essentially divine!

When you grow in this awareness, you identify yourself with the Everlasting. You begin to say to yourself, "I am not this body. I am the *atman*, the deathless spirit. My spirit is the Universe. My essence is of God."

This realisation releases a tremendous energy of the spirit within you, that it can transform your life and your personality completely! Aware of the divine within you, you begin to recognise and respect the divinity in others, and your consciousness expands; you become more understanding, more tolerant, more loving and forgiving, more magnanimous – in short, more divine than human!

Identification with the *atman* is not merely of abstract value. In practical terms, it can make life joyous, peaceful and secure. I often narrate to my friends, the story of the Persian king who had his ring inscribed with the words: *This too shall pass away.* When he read these words, he gained equanimity and wisdom. He was no longer unduly elated by good news – nor did defeat and bad news depress his spirits. He had learnt the secret that the world is transient, changing – and therefore, it is futile to cling to changing objects and changing events.

This too shall pass away. Nothing is permanent. Alone, the soul abides!

Build your life in the Atman-
the Rock of the Ages. And
the Atman is reached
through silence.
And the Atman , is silence!
Shantooyam Atman!

In Quest of the Self

Let me begin with a simple story.

A farmer found an eagle's egg atop a hill; he brought it to his farm and put it with the rest of the eggs in the nest of a barnyard hen. The eaglet hatched along with the brood of chicks and grew up with them in the barnyard.

All his life the eagle did whatever the barnyard chicks did, for he thought that he too, was a barnyard chicken. He scratched the earth for worms and insects. He clucked and cackled like his 'siblings'. And occasionally, he would thrash his wings and fly a few feet up into the air, and be very pleased with his efforts.

Years passed and the eagle was now very old. One day, as he was shuffling about in the farmyard, he saw a shadow fall over him; he looked up and saw a magnificent bird hovering above him in the blue sky. It was gliding gracefully, effortlessly, in the powerful wind currents, borne aloft on its strong golden wings.

The old eagle was awestruck. "What's that?" he asked.

"That's the eagle, the king of the birds, the lord of the skies" said his neighbour. "He belongs to the sky. We belong to the earth – we're chickens."

The eagle lived and died a chicken, for he never really knew who he was.

If you would progress on the path of self-realisation, you must stop identifying yourself with the body. You must move away from the "shoes" you wear. This is indeed the significance of the custom practised by Hindus – removing one's shoes before one enters a temple or a holy place. This is symbolic of the idea that we move away from body-consciousness to walk upon the sanctified ground, which will help us move towards God-realisation.

We cannot cast off the body, literally. But we can change our perspective by dwelling on the idea that we are not the bodies we wear – we are the immortal spirits within. This makes a tremendous change in the outlook!

The human birth has invested us with a body-mind complex; but the body-mind are just instruments to aid our existence here; the truth is the indwelling spirit.

How far are you swayed by external appearances?

Whom would you respect and revere and welcome to your house – a man who arrives in a Benz? A man who arrives on a two-wheeler, or a man who walks in simply?

How much importance do you attach to people's appearance, the clothes they wear and the accessories/jewels they wear on their person?

If you give truthful answers to these questions, you will know how far you have progressed on the path of self-knowledge.

The truth, as I have been repeatedly saying to you is this: you are the immortal spirit! You are a spark of the Divine!

In his serene and quiet *ashram* on the banks of the River Yamuna, a Guru was addressing a group of his disciples.

"The spark of the Divine is within you," he said to the young seekers. "You are an aspect of the Divine. You must constantly aspire to perfection; to be perfect is to be God-like."

One of the disciples was puzzled by the remark. He stood up and said to the Guru, "But sire, God is great. He is omnipotent, omnipresent and omniscient. Infinite worlds exist within Him. How can we ever hope to be like God?"

The Guru said to him, "Here is my water bowl. Take it to the Yamuna River and fill it with water."

The disciple left, and in a few minutes he was back with a filled bowl. The Guru looked at the bowl and said, "This is not the water from the Yamuna. I told you to get water from the Yamuna River."

"I beg your pardon, Guruji," said the disciple. "This is indeed water from the Yamuna River. I did exactly what you told me to do."

"I tell you, this cannot be water from the Yamuna," insisted the Guru. "There are fish and turtles in the Yamuna; there are cows standing in the river; there are people bathing in its waters. Where are the fish in this bowl? Where are the turtles and cows? Why, there isn't a single person bathing here! And you tell me this is the water of the Yamuna River? Go and get me the water of the Yamuna River."

The disciple was taken aback. "But Guruji," he stammered. "I brought just a bowl full of water from the Yamuna for you. How can a bowl contain all those things you mention?"

"True, a little bowl can't contain all those things," agreed the Guru. "Now go and pour this water back into the Yamuna."

The disciple went and poured the water into the river, and returned.

"Tell me, don't all those things exist in that water now?" the Guru asked him. "See for yourself, the fish, the turtles, the cows and the people; they are all in the river, aren't they? The individual soul is like the water in the bowl. It is one with God, but it exists in a limited form, and therefore it seems to be very different from God. When you poured the water from the bowl into the river, that water once again contained fish, turtles, cows, and everything else that the river contains. In the same way, when you see your own inner Self through meditation and knowledge, you will realise that you are That and that your spirit pervades everywhere, just like God. Once you are aware of this, you will know that you are an aspect of God!"

The Vedas tell us: *nityo nityanam chetanas chetananam:* the Lord is the chief individual living entity, the leader of the subordinate living entities. Thus the presence of the Divine spark in all creation is suggested; qualitatively the supreme being and the individual soul are the same; quantitatively, God is infinite power and knowledge; we are limited beings; the analogy used is that of the ocean and a drop of water from it. Because the living entities are parts or samples of God, their qualities are not different from those of the Supreme Lord.

The word *atman*, originating from Sanskrit and having Indo Germanic links, is translated also as "essence, breath or soul". In Hindu philosophy, it is regarded as the first principle of being, the true self. Older Upanishads such as the *Brihadaranyaka*, mention several times that the Self is described as *Neti Neti* or "not this - not this".

Lord Sri Krishna too, confirms this in his Avadhuta Gita: "By such *vakyas* as "That thou art," our own Self is affirmed. Of that which is untrue and composed of the five elements - the *Sruti* (scripture) says, *Neti, Neti* "Not this, not this".

There is such a thing as definition by negation: you can grasp certain concepts by understanding clearly what they are *not*. This works especially with abstract and complex concepts. Thus poverty is absence of wealth. Sadness or depression is the absence of joy. In this sense, negation becomes what we call a logical complement, defining a thing by what it is not.

Neti! Neti! This is nothing but a definition by negation. The *atma* is not something we can grasp with the senses and the Mind; it is beyond the senses and the Mind!

"All that is, is physical and material," an atheist writes. "There is no Soul. Your mind is the subjective experience of what the molecules in your brain cells are doing. Galileo kicked us out of the Center of the Universe. Darwin kicked us off the Pinnacle of Creation. Freud kicked the Soul out of our Brains. There is nothing more to life than materialism."

"Can someone tell me where exactly in the human body the soul is located?" asks another young man in doubt. "Is there an area of the brain, a structure that corresponds to the soul?"

All I can say in response to the above is this: until recently, scientists believed that the atom was indivisible and indestructible...now we know differently.

In the wise words of the Chinese sage, Lao Tse, It is only when I let go of what I am, that I can become what I might be.

Spirituality is a value; it is an attitude to life; an approach to the purpose of existence. If some of you are content to live life at the material level, and have no needs beyond the sensual, the material and the emotional – well, there's an end of the matter!

But as we have been discussing all this while, none of us is content with the material level of existence. All of us, laymen and women, students and working professionals, businessmen and managers, young and old are deeply concerned about their holistic growth as human beings. Everybody is concerned about their inner life; everyone craves for a sense of peace and harmony that is central to their being. We may not want to renounce the world to find that elusive peace; but we are ready and willing to spend some time focusing our attention on the rich interior world that is within us. We continue our quest for the soul as best we can...

A friend demonstrated to me the security settings on his laptop, which operates on a face recognition software. Until and unless his own face appeared before the camera built into the computer, the machine could not be 'opened' nor its data accessed by another.

If this is the unique feature of the human visage, then imagine for yourself the unique nature of the human spirit!

"The *Atman* is subtler than the subtlest and not to be known through argument," so the *Katha Upanishad* tells us.

The *Isha Upanishad* states, "If you remove a part from infinity or add a part to infinity, what remains is still infinity".

That is whole, this is whole,

From the whole the whole arises

When the whole is taken from the whole,

The whole will still remain.

The question then arises: How is the *atman* unique to each one of us, if it is, as we said, a spark of the Divine? When a soul assumes a human body in a specific birth or *janma*, it takes up its new birth at that stage of spiritual evolution which it reached in its previous human birth and continues to evolve towards *atma-saakshatkara* or Self-realisation in its current birth. In other words, spirituality is unique and different for each one of us, because our souls are at different stages of evolution towards ultimate self-knowledge and Liberation.

Most spiritual traditions teach us that knowing the true Self is the equivalent of actually knowing God. For God is immanent in all creation; He is the Indweller in every soul; so knowledge of the Self is knowledge of the Indweller, the *antaryami* who resides within all of us. In other words, spirituality, or the quest to discover the nature of one's own highest consciousness, is in essence, the quest to discover God.

But there is a practical aspect to this quest for the spirit that I wish to emphasise. It is said that God 'pierced' our five senses so that they are constantly tuned to the outer reality, and therefore, cannot grapple with what is within us. But the senses can be controlled, so that the mind and consciousness can be focused within. In this sense, the search for the *atman* is a discipline – essentially, self-discipline.

Through the process of negation that I spoke of earlier, we may arrive at what this quest for the *atman* is all about. Here again, I must emphasise, it is different for each one of us:

1. It is essentially a quest for self-discovery
2. It is choosing what you would want your true self to be and become
3. It is an attempt to go beyond the external world of materialism
4. It is a desire to transcend the ego, its limitations, its fears and insecurities
5. It is an effort to discover/ understand the unity of all creation
6. It is the knowledge that I and my fellow human beings and my fellow creatures are part of the One Whole
7. It is uniquely personal and yet emphasises the interconnectedness of all creation
8. It is an aspiration to discover and fulfill the purpose of human existence
9. It is discovering the power of love, compassion and respect – nay, reverence for all forms of life.
10. It is the awareness that there is more to your life than worldly success and achievements
11. It is discovering the Divine within you – and within all creation
12. It is discovering true joy, peace and contentment
13. Spirituality means something different to each seeker
14. At its best, it is yoga – union with God

May I share with you a fivefold teaching that I received in my youth from an unknown saint? These valuable lessons taught me to move away, gradually, from identifying myself with the body: these are the first steps that all of us must take when we set out in quest of the spirit:

- Remember, that you are a pilgrim here, a wayfarer in quest of your lost homeland. Your Home is in Eternity
- Be patient in the midst of the difficulties and dangers of life. Remind yourself again and again, "This too shall pass away!"
- Each day meditate on death, for death approaches us with each passing moment
- Give the service of love to all
- Seek fellowship with saints and holy men so that the tiny drop that you are may become a mighty ocean, wide enough to hold within it a thousand oceans

As long as we remain unaware of this great truth — that the soul is eternal, and that the body is mortal — we become obsessed with the physical, material and sensual aspects of life.

The Wonder That Is The Soul

Let me begin with the rousing call of the Gita so beautifully adapted by Swami Vivekananda: Awake! Arise! Search your real self!

Look within and ask yourself, what am I? What is the truth of my being?

The *Shrimad Bhagwat* describes the soul as a wonder. It is the ultimate, infinite wonder. The more you ponder over it, the more you will be fascinated by it! Once you realise that you are the *Atman*, once you attain self-realisation, you will be free from all worldly bonds; you will be free from fear and insecurity. You will be like a bird soaring high in the sky.

Self-realisation makes you aware of the Oneness of all life, the Oneness of this vast Universe. It teaches us that Man and God are one in essence! This is the Truth. This is the knowledge. This is what man has to discover for himself.

Let me take you back to the time when the Sikh Gurus lived in this ancient land of ours. It was a time when the country was torn by strife between the Moghul Rulers and their Hindu subjects. There are many references to this strife in the sacred *bani* of Guru Nanak.

At the time I speak of, Shah Jahan had been dethroned and imprisoned by his younger son Aurangzeb, who usurped the Moghul throne. Crown Prince Dara Shikoh had to flee from the court, and on his way to Lahore, came to seek the blessings of the Seventh Guru, Guru Har Rai, at Goindwal. The meeting was reported to Aurangzeb, and the Guru was summoned to the court.

But the Guru was not inclined to accept the summons. "I rule over no territory, I owe the king no tax," he said to the messengers, "nor do I want anything from him. There is no connection of teacher and disciple between us, either. Of what avail will this meeting be?"

However, he sent his elder son, Ram Rai as his representative to answer the summons. He blessed his young son as he seated him in the carriage and exhorted him: "Answer squarely and without fear any questions the Emperor may ask. Exhibit no hesitation. Read the *Granth* attentively as you make halts on the way. The Guru will protect you wherever you might be."

Few of us know of Ram Rai; he was also a *tapasvi* in his own right. He too was a '*sadhak*'. He had mastered many '*siddhis*' (extra-ordinary feats). Ram Rai obeyed his father and went to the court of Mughal Emperor Aurangzeb and presented himself. He was first met by the Emperor's *Maulvi* and *Kazi*; they asked him to perform a miracle. Ram Rai with his knowledge of *siddhis*, performed many miracles. It is said he performed 22 *siddhis* in the court of Aurangzeb!

The *Maulvi* and the *Kazi* were stunned! They had hoped to implicate him as a traitor and an impious man before the Emperor, so that the growing power of Sikhism could be curbed. But the young man was beyond reproach. Desperate to find fault with the young man on any account, they said to the Emperor, "Your Majesty! The Sikhs have made a sacred scripture called their *Granth*. In the *Granth* they have abused Musalmans. In the *Granth*, it is written, "*Mitti Musalman ki, pere pai ghumiar*".

It is reported that Aurangzeb put Ram Rai through several tests; the Guru's son managed to pass them all. But when he was asked to interpret one of the lines from Guru Nanak's *shabads*, it is said that the young man deliberately distorted their meaning, for he was fearful that the Guru's words would be unacceptable to the temperamental and fanatical emperor.

In short, it happened thus: Aurangzeb wanted to satisfy himself that there was nothing against Islam written in the Holy Granth. He asked Ram Rai to explain why Guru Nanak had said:

Mitti Musalman ki, pere pai ghumiar,
Ghar bhande itan kian, jahdi kale pukar.

"The ashes of Moslems find their way into the potter's clod,

Pots and bricks are made out of them, they cry out as they're fired."

Ram Rai was unnerved. He forgot his father's instructions and said, on an impulse, "Your Majesty, Guru Nanak wrote *'Mitti Beiman Ki'* and not *'Mitti Musalman ki'*; that is 'the ashes of the faithless,' not of the Moslems' fall into the potter's clod. Someone has distorted the original text. It seems to have been done to slander both Islam and Sikhism."

Of course, Aurangzeb was mightily pleased with this 'diplomatic' interpretation. He offered a hand of friendship to the young Sikh leader and sent him away with gifts and honours.

We know what transpired later. When word reached the Guru that his son had misinterpreted the scriptures in order to escape the wrath of the emperor, he was deeply saddened. Ram Rai was debarred from his father's presence. He was not permitted to enter Kiratpur ever again. He pleaded repeatedly for forgiveness, but his father was unrelenting. Thus Guru Har Rai established a strict propriety and absolute respect for the scriptures, against any alteration of the original verses.

Every word spoken by Guru Nanak is sacred. Every word from his *bani* is radiant with truth and wisdom. The above words from the Guru's *bani* have great significance, when we look at the context of their utterance. Guru Nanak spoke these words when he met the grandson of the great Sufi Mystic, Shaikh Farid. Farid's grandson had a 'mystical' dialogue with Guru Nanak. He uttered the prophetic words: "When there is a battle between two nations, and when a person (Hindu) is killed, his body is burnt and reduced to ashes. Many walk over it, and in doing so, crunch the ashes under their heels."

To this Guru Nanak replied, "Same is the fate of Muslims, when a Muslim dies, he is buried, and finally merges with mud. The potter takes that mud and makes pots out of it."

The point that the Guru made was this: it is futile to divide humanity by the rites of burial or cremation, as practised by different faiths; whether it is a Hindu or a Mussalman, ultimately their physical bodies are destroyed and become dust. This utterance reminds us of the truth that our bodies are perishable; they will turn to dust and ashes when we die. But the soul within is immortal, indestructible.

Ram Rai was perforce made to stay away from his father. However, he continued with his *'sadhana'*. He continued to enjoy imperial patronage. He was granted a *jagir* in the Garhwal hills, where he established his *Dera* or missionary centre, in the Doon valley, which is known as Dehra Dun today. He continued to preach the gospel of Guru Nanak, and developed his own sect of followers known as the Ramraias. The Ramraias still form a dissident sect of the Udasi Sikhs.

There is yet another legend about Ram Rai's *siddhis*, that has been handed down to us. Once, a devotee living in Peshawar sent him a 'distress call'. Saints often solve the difficulties of their devotees, by visiting them in their ethereal or astral form. To put it in simple terms, they are high voltage 'sensors' who answer the call of their devotees wherever they happen to be. They leave their bodies and go to help the devotee. Ram Rai said to his wife, "I am leaving my body and going to Peshawar. Do not allow anyone to touch my body. I will finish my work and return at an appropriate time and re-enter the body."

Ram Rai, in his astral form, went to Peshawar and helped his devotee. But during his absence, a few *masands* happened to visit his house. *Masands* are messengers of Guru Nanak, who travel far and wide spreading the Guru's message of peace and harmony. The *Masands* forcibly touched the body of Ram Rai and found it lifeless; thereupon, they decided to take it to the cremation ground and burn it. When Ram Rai returned home, he found that his body had been taken away. His wife felt his astral presence. Ram Rai asked her, "Where is my body?"

The wife replied that the *Masands* had taken it away and cremated it.

Today, many parapsychologists and mystics treat OOBE or out-of-body-experiences as reported by some people as evidence of the truth of the soul.

Many of us may not have had such experiences. But surely some of us have felt that we are not 'there' but elsewhere. Near-death experiences also cause us to feel that we can detach ourselves from our physical bodies and 'look on' ourselves, as if from a distance. In a book titled *The Ultimate Guide to What Happens When We Die,* the author describes such experiences narrated by people who recovered from the verge of death.

Many pious people believe that during deep meditation or the stage of deep sleep at night, our 'souls' leave the body and go out to seek the holy one on a Divine plane.

Once, one of our *satsangi* sisters met a lady theosophist, who was a very pious and devout believer. This lady said to her, "We have met before, haven't we?"

The sister shook her head and replied politely, "I don't think so."

The lady was herself a practitioner of aura therapy. She could read the aura of a person and also 'look' into the person's past and present by touching his or her pulse. In India, we had developed many such 'mystical' sciences, which are now unfortunately lost to us under the onslaught of the technological and rational tendencies of today.

The theosophist told this girl, "Of course we have met before. We met at Mont Blanc. We have met several times. You may not remember it!"

Our girl from the *satsang* was rational. She came to me and asked several questions about these 'Out Of Body Experiences'.

I told her, ".We do not know or remember them, because our souls travel while our brain is in sleep."

Friends, you too can remember your astral travels when you reach the level of Deep Meditation where your consciousness touches the super consciousness. Then there is Oneness. In that Oneness you discover things, which are beyond description. They are beyond words.

There is a lady called Anita Moorjani who has written a book titled *Dying to Be Me: My Journey from Cancer, to Near Death, to True Healing*. In this fascinating book, she records her losing battle with cancer over a four year period, at the end of which she had a near-death experience. This changed her life dramatically: when she recovered consciousness, her condition improved rapidly and she was discharged from hospital within four weeks. During this OOBE, Anita had a mystic vision where she learnt all about illness, healing, fear, "being love", and the true magnificence of each and every human being! She asserts the case that we are essentially spiritual beings having a human experience, and that we are all One.

To discover this principle of oneness is to discover the truth of the *atman*. Dear friends, I urge you to search within. Search for your real self, the immortal self. Search for the truth. Go within! Look for the *Atman* within. 'Know thyself' say the scriptures. 'Cultivate the soul!' says Gurudev Sadhu Vaswani.

How do I realise my 'Self', my true being? This is the question often put to me. Here are a few simple practical suggestions.

1. Get up early in the morning preferably around five o'clock. Between 3 and 5 o'clock is what we call '*Brahma Mahurat*'. During this period *Sattvic* vibrations are present all around us. This helps the mind to be in tune with the inner self. Set aside at least 45 minutes for meditation. Begin

meditation either with a chant or a silent prayer. Then observe silence as long as you can.
2. In the state of God consciousness, there is no within or without. However, you may meditate on the form within your heart, i.e. the special deity with whom you are linked, whether it be Shiva, Krishna, Christ, Guru Nanak or any other symbol which connects you to spirituality or to higher consciousness.
3. Many people tell me that thoughts of the external world disturb the silence and distract your concentration. Let thoughts come and go. Do not dwell on thoughts, think of them as water stored in a dam. The breeze brings waves; waves come and go but the water remains as it is.
4. Be compassionate towards all beings. *Ahimsa* is the highest *Dharma*. Compassion will also lead you to adopt a vegetarian diet – which is *sattvic* food.
5. Spend some time in reading inspirational literature.
6. Be in fellowship with nature.
7. Be in fellowship with the holy ones; be in the *satsang* as often as you can.
8. Be rooted in Truth. Do not speak lies. Avoid people who are negative, critical of others; or those puffed with pride.
9. Forgive every one. Forgive yourself also.
10. Discipline, regularity and sincerity are very necessary on the path of self-realisation.
11. Finally, humility and modesty alone will take you to your goal. A seed does not sprout by itself. It goes into the soil, merges with the soil, before it grows and bears fruit. Humility and sacrifice are a must on the path of the spiritual aspirant.

My dear ones, when you follow these suggestions, your life will be transformed. You will feel peace within you. You will enjoy God's creation. You will also want to go out and help others. May be, a day will come in your life, when you will be 'sensors' to 'distress calls' and you will become God's instruments of help and healing. And then you will sparkle with the radiance of the Divine.

We would miss some of the best blessings of life, if suffering did not come to us. Suffering is a great teacher.

The Gift of Sorrow

Gurudev Sadhu Vaswani has given us a profound message in one of his poems which is like a prayer. 'In all circumstances and under all conditions, in sorrow and suffering remember that God knows the best. Whatever he does is for our benefit. What may seem to us, to be an obstacle, a difficulty, or just misfortune, has been sent to us with a definite purpose. Whatever happens to us, whatever befalls us, has a hidden meaning, which we are often unable to see or comprehend'.

Some time ago, a girl came to meet me. She is a true devotee of the Lord. She has for long cherished an intense yearning to have His vision. She is a true seeker. She said to me, "Ever since I have kindled this flame of yearning for the Lord, I have had to face many problems and difficulties. In fact, I can say that I have never felt as lonely as under these situations. I have felt darkness around me."

I said to her, "You are indeed the fortunate one, because it is these experiences which will make you realise your higher self. These situations of loneliness, of being left out, will carve a special path for you, to reach your goal, your goal of self-realisation!"

Gurudev Sadhu Vaswani said to us: "Blessed is the Truth seeker. For his life is tragedy and tears." Every suffering is a gift from God. It is the gift that will help you in self growth. To avoid suffering is to shut yourself away from The Life Beautiful. The supreme vision of Beauty comes from the cross!

Sorrow, grief, hardship, loneliness and insecurities are given to us to make us strong in spirit, to endow us with moral courage, or what I call muscles of the spirit. Difficulties give us courage and strengthen our will power. They put us through a process of cleansing and purification.

That reminds me again of the words of my Gurudev. Long ago, we were sitting out with him in an open courtyard in Hyderabad Sind. It was a clear starry night, and we felt blessed to be in his presence. He said to us, "Saints come into this world to do the job of a *dhobi*. They come here to wash you, cleanse you, remove all the filth accumulated over your previous births and make you clean and pure and radiant and ready to enter His presence."

My dear brothers and sisters, we have been collecting the accumulated impurities, the *vasanas* of past lives which are to the soul like household dust, filth and muck, over the cycle of previous births. It is difficult; nay, it is impossible for an individual working on his own to remove those layers of filth.

It is only the Guru, who is a man of God, who can do this for us.

While we were on this topic, Gurudev Sadhu Vaswani's spiritual daughter, Sister Shanti said, impulsively and spontaneously, "Gurudev, will you wash me? Will you cleanse me?" Shanti was a child of God; and she strived to live a pure life.

Gurudev Sadhu Vaswani smiled and said, "Why not, if you want to be cleansed, I shall do it."

Shanti wanted to confirm and be assured, so she said, "Gurudev, I beg you to promise me!"

And to this Gurudev Sadhu Vaswani replied, "Yes, my dear, it's a promise!"

From that day onwards, Shanti had to face many difficult situations. She had to face many challenges. Shanti became sad and depressed; she would often spend sleepless nights, shedding secret tears in her room.

Shanti was a favourite child of Gurudev Sadhu Vaswani. He loved her immensely. But, from the day that she had made the request to him to cleanse her and purify her, Gurudev avoided her. We did not realise it then, but he was putting her to the test, strengthening her moral fibre!

Many days passed, and Shanti endured indescribable pain, for a true disciple lives and moves by the Guru's grace and draws her will and strength to live from his loving gaze and his sacred presence. To Shanti, deliberately distanced from this spiritual nourishment, it must have been like being cut off from oxygen!

She could take it no more! And one day Shanti plucked up enough courage to go and sit at his feet. She began to cry. "Gurudev, please tell me, where have I gone wrong? What is it that I have done to offend you? Please forgive me if I have failed you in any way. I am unable to bear your indifference towards me."

Gurudev Sadhu Vaswani was all compassion, and it had never been his intention to hurt her. Lovingly, he said to her, "Dear Shanti, you had asked me to do the *dhobi's* job of cleansing you. I was merely washing. The one who wishes to be cleansed accepts every difficulty, every unpleasant situation, and all suffering as His *prasad*."

Each one of us has to go through the experience of suffering; hence we must learn to accept suffering as a part of growing up. Learn to value suffering, because there can be no self-growth without suffering.

The Guru, let us remember, is omniscient; he knows us perhaps better than we know ourselves. Then why does he allow us to be put to a test of our spiritual mettle? Why does he need to see if we have imbibed his teachings well?

The answer is simple: to show us exactly where we stand; and, perhaps, to show the others what our true potential is.

The Guru, Sadhu Vaswani taught us, is much more than an 'instructor' or 'advisor'. He is a dynamic person with a transforming power – for spirituality is a tremendous *shakti;* and the true Guru is a man of *shakti*. By the method of evocation, the Guru draws out the disciple's spiritual energy. Therefore we read in the ancient texts: "The Guru leads forth the pupil to Himself!" It is in this process of 'leading forth', drawing the disciple to Himself – not in merely communicating information – lies the secret of the Guru's *shakti*.

Guru-*bhakti* involves unconditional surrender, absolute faith and devoted service to the Guru; this naturally includes utter obedience to the Guru's wishes, bearing witness to his teachings in deeds of daily living.

To put it briefly, every word we utter, every action we perform, every thought we think, each and every reaction we offer to external circumstances must bear witness to the guru's teachings. We are not sages or saints, like the Masters; nor are we evolved beings who have seen the light; but we are, and we must ever remain true seekers – seekers after spiritual growth, seekers after perfection, seekers after eventual liberation.

Seekers like us cannot get away with pass marks in the test of life! Perfection, or at least excellence should be our hallmark.

"Excuse me," some of you may feel like interjecting at this point, "but why should we be put to a test of pain and suffering? Isn't that harsh and strict and unkind?"

On the other hand, it is only God's kindness and the Guru's great concern for us that puts these tests before us – it is so that we understand ourselves, grow in self-realisation and develop spiritual strength. In other words, it is for our own spiritual well-being. Taking these spiritual tests will see us grow in wisdom, understanding and faith.

May I share with you my own experience of suffering? Behind every suffering that afflicts us, is the shadow of God himself. God wears the cloak of suffering and comes to us to cleanse our life. Those who know this truth, welcome suffering. Those who do not know this truth complain. They reject the very idea of suffering being good for spiritual progress! They scoff at teachers who tell them that suffering and pain purify the body and the soul. It is very similar to the process by which your washing machine soaks, churns, rolls about, rinses and wrings your clothes dry to cleanse them!

There is a little known story about Kunti, told to us in our ancient books: Once Sri Krishna granted her a boon to ask for whatever she wanted. What she wanted was indeed strange! She said to the Lord, "Lord, give me a little suffering all the time. For I have come to realise that in pleasures and enjoyments, You are often forgotten. But in pain and suffering, You are always remembered."

Kunti was right. Today, many of us enjoy the luxuries of life, many of us have a comfortable living. When everything goes right we forget God, we feel we can manage our lives perfectly well without His help; well, we may remember the Lord in passing, as we mutter a few prayers mechanically; but we are alright without Him! We get on with our lives. We are too busy, too involved, too wrapped up in our worldly activities to remember Him!

But the moment things start going wrong, the moment difficulties strike, we turn to God with alacrity. We call out to Him to come to our aid. As Sant Kabir points out, we do not need God when the going is good. We need him only in suffering, we remember him in difficulties; we remember him when we are in trouble.

It is the nature of lesser mortals like us to try and run away from all suffering and unpleasant experiences.

"I wish, I would disappear!" we moan. "I wish I could just run away from it all!"

Such painful experiences, I would like to tell you, are essential to our spiritual growth. God wants us to face them and grow in moral and spiritual strength. The best way to face such difficult situations, is not merely to accept them, but cooperate with their inner purpose, fixing our minds and hearts – not on the pain and difficulties we face – but on Him who has planned it all for us.

Suffering, I think, is of two types: the first is unnecessary suffering, which we create for ourselves through wrong thinking and wrong feeling. The second type of suffering comes to us from God: it comes to the best of men, the noblest of souls. It came to Krishna and Christ, to Buddha and Zoroaster, to Moses and Prophet Mohammed, to Nanak and Kabir, to Ramakrishna Paramahansa and Sadhu Vaswani. This type of suffering does not come alone; it brings with itself the strength, which endures, the comfort which lends sweetness to the suffering.

The suffering which man brings on himself, is hard and unbearable. (Most of us will realise that this is how we felt when we have passed through trials.) When we do not respond to life's incidents and accidents in the right attitude, it can break our spirit and throw us in an abyss of gloom. But if we are able to cast all thoughts of self aside, and behold the loving hand of God in every condition and circumstance of life, we have a positive answer to the question: why did this have to happen?

We realise that everything that happens, happens for our good. Everything that comes to pass is the result of God's infinite goodness and unfailing love for us! Therefore, I often recite this prayer:

>Thou know'st everything, Beloved,
>Let Thy Will always be done!
>In joy and sorrow, my Beloved,
>Let Thy Will always be done!

When we take things personally, selfishly, when we feel that we are the victims of God's unfair, unjust ways, even a little pain becomes hard to bear. But when we accept pain and suffering as God's Will for us, He takes up our burden, and the yoke becomes easy to bear!

May I give you words of the German mystic, Meister Eckhart: "Believe me, if there was a man who was willing to suffer on account of God and God alone, then though he fell a sudden prey to all the collective sufferings of the world, it would not trouble nor bow him down, for God would be the bearer of his burden."

It was said of Jesus, when He suffered intense pain and agony on the cross: "He came to save others; how is it that He cannot save Himself?"

That remark was obviously made in ignorance; for suffering is a gift consciously chosen and willingly accepted by saviours and saints, helpers and healers of humanity.

As Gurudev Sadhu Vaswani puts it so beautifully: "Suffering is the benediction which God pours upon His beloved children to whom He would reveal the meaning of His Infinite mercy – reveal Himself, His wisdom and His love!"

Saints and holy men receive the arrows of pain as gifts from the all-giver. Alike in sunshine and in rain, they rejoice, give gratitude to God and sing His Holy Name. Every great one of humanity has had to bear his cross.

We know that Sri Ramakrishna Paramahansa, during his final days, was afflicted with acute pain and suffering due to cancer of the throat. Despite the severe pain and inability to talk, he constantly spoke to his devotees of God and spirituality. He could eat very little; but his joy and radiance were infectious. During these days of affliction, some of his devotees, unable to see his suffering due to the advanced stage of the throat cancer, begged him to cure himself through the power of prayer. The saint agreed to do this, smiling gently. But sometime later, he sent word for Swami Vivekananda and told him that he had indeed asked Mother Kali to help him overcome his inability to swallow food; but, he said to his dear devoted disciple, that the Divine Mother drew his attention to all the people in the *Ashram* and in the outside world, and asked him if he was not eating through all their mouths!

The truth is that Sri Ramakrishna's consciousness was no longer tethered to the shell of his own physical body. He had transcended the physical aspect of pain and suffering!

Let us thank God for suffering- it teaches us courage.
Let us thank God for disappointments - they teach us to be ready for His appointment!

Whatever Happens, Happens for the Best

It is said that when the Sufi mystic Rabia was in great affliction, one of her friends urged her to ask God for relief from pain. Rabia's answer was significant: she said to him, "Do you not know who it is that wills this suffering for me? Is it not God who wills it? Why then do you bid me ask for something that is contrary to His Will? It is not well to oppose one's beloved."

In a passage of unsurpassed beauty, Shah Abdul Latif, the beloved poet of Sind, exclaims: "I have known of no one who met the Beloved in happiness!" Indeed, the Law of Love is the Law of the Cross, the Law of Suffering and Sacrifice.

The first Sufi saints were called "those who always weep" and "those who see this world as a hut of sorrows". "Little food, little talk, little sleep", was a popular proverb amongst them. Mortification of the flesh, self-denial, poverty and abstinence were seen by them as the means of drawing near to God, and this included fasting and long nights of prayer. The Sufis saw all suffering and pain as a means of drawing closer to God, their Beloved.

A holy woman tells us that the Lord appeared to her one day, and said: "I bring to you three gifts; choose the one you like the most!"

The three gifts she discovered, did indeed present tough choices – they were undeserved criticism, disease and persecution.

The saint weighed the three gifts and found that each was more difficult to accept than the remaining two. "To be criticised for no fault of mine! To be called a bad character, a thief, a liar, a hypocrite, when I am actually innocent . . .? To become a victim to a disease, to lie in bed, unable to move, unable to get up, perhaps unable to speak, and be in this condition month after month, year after year . . .? To be treated as a criminal when my life is spotless, to be persecuted, flogged, terribly tortured...?"

All the three seemed unbearable, and she trembled as she thought of what would happen if she chose any of the three gifts.

The Lord smiled and, in His extended hand, were the three gifts. As she looked up into His tender, smiling face, something happened to her and, unhesitatingly she said, "Lord, I take all the three!"

When we bleed and are in pain, let us remember that the Will of God is working through us: and through suffering and pain, God's will is purifying us, preparing for the Vision of Light!

I was witness to the great pain and agony that my beloved Master went through in the final days of his earth-journey.

Gurudev Sadhu Vaswani lay ill and in great pain. He had passed a restless night: and though his eyelids were heavy with sleep, the shooting pains all over his body would not let him sleep for over a minute or two at a time. I had watched him throughout the night and had seen how even when the pain was acute, he continued to smile. When the pain became unbearable, out of his parted lips came one word: "*Shukur*! *Shukur*! Gratitude to Thee, O Lord of Mercy!"

His feeble body was so broken with illness and pain that it was a wonder how he could bear it. I, also, wondered that this prince amongst men, this man of singular purity and prayer, service and sacrifice, who would not hurt an ant, and who gave the love of his gentle, generous heart to all – the rich and the poor, the young and the old, the sinner and the saint – and who loved birds and animals and every flower of the field and every lotus in the lake and every atom of matter and every ray of light – I wondered that such a man should have to suffer so terribly.

Through Gurudev Sadhu Vaswani, healing had flowed to many who were sick and afflicted. Now, when he was in the throes of pain, nothing could be done to give him relief! The doctors were helpless. We, who were near him, could only wake and watch and shed hidden tears of sorrow. But all the while he rejoiced in his heart that, by making him endure great agony of body, God was using him to heal others.

One night, at about three o' clock, finding it difficult to bear the sight of his suffering, I said to him: "Beloved! You are a friend of God. Why will you not pray to Him that He may heal you of this illness which your feeble body is unable to bear? Surely God will listen to your prayers!"

Quietly, he answered: "To me, my child, there is nothing sweeter than the Will of the Lord. And if it be His Will that I suffer, such suffering is sweeter to me than relief from pain: for, verily, in the fulfillment of His Holy Will is my real comfort and solace!" After a brief while, with uplifted eyes, he prayed: "Gratitude to Thee, my God and my Lord, for this gift of pain. And if it be Thy Will to add to it tenfold, I pray Thee to do so without delay. In Thy Will alone is the peace I seek!"

And the Master added: "I know not much. I only know that there is suffering in the world. And men and women wander in the darkness. In such a world let me go about giving love and compassion to all. Let me serve the poor and broken ones, serve my brothers and sisters, serve birds and beasts and all creatures in whom is the One breath of life. Let me not waste energy in questions or controversies. Let me light a few candles at the altar of suffering creation."

I have seen that saints often take on their sufferings gladly: one reason for this is that they wish to 'settle' their *karmic* accounts, and become liberated from the cycle of death and rebirth. The second is that they are profoundly compassionate by nature, and so they are willing to take on the pain and suffering of others. For them, bodily suffering has no significance. They do suffer, but once it is past, they do not even retain a memory of it. Thus it was that Sri Ramana Maharishi, Sri Ramakrishna and Gurudev Sadhu Vaswani, underwent a great deal of pain and suffering in their last years...

"Do they actually feel all that pain, or do they simply transcend their suffering?" someone asked me once.

I said to them, "Pain is real and actual, for everyone. Some of the saints actually suffer far more than the rest, because their bodies are very sensitive and their consciousness is profound."

A holy man who, for many years, was active in the service of God and His suffering children, said with candid simplicity: "Lord, You have cheated me! When I offered myself to Your service, I felt that all I would receive would be tears, hunger, starvation, perspiration, vexation, oppression, persecution, pain. But You have given me the sweetest comfort. I feel cheated, Lord! But it is a happy misunderstanding."

Guru Nanak was a practical saint; people from near and far would come to have his *darshan* and blessings.

Sometimes Guru Nanak would ask the devotees seeking blessings, "What kind of blessings do you want- first, second or third?"

Hearing this, the devotees would be baffled. They would think; do blessings also have numbers? So they would ask, "Lord! We do not understand what you say?"

Guru Nanak would reply, "If you want blessing number one, then you will suffer losses in business. If you want blessing number two, then you will lose all your wealth. And, if you want blessing number three, then you will have to take a begging bowl to get few pieces of bread; which you may or may not get!"

The devotees would be appalled at this and tell Guru Nanak, "Lord, we thought Blessings are to be bestowed on us, and not meant to take away from what we have!"

To this Guru Nanak would reply, "You will get something, which is more precious and valuable than these worldly trinkets."

My dear brothers and sisters, saints come to this world to bear witness to truth. But we human beings are so involved in our worldly affairs that we fail to see the truth. The one who has tasted the divine nectar will be indifferent to the worldly pleasures, because the worldly pleasures are bitter. They are the cause of unhappiness. The true happiness or the true bliss comes with experiencing the divine.

The Lord's injunction to us is quite clear: "Go to the great ones," He tells us. "Surrender to them; devote yourself to them; ask of them; and they will impart the knowledge to you."

The teachings of all the great ones is consistent with Truth. If at all there are any contradictions, they exist only in our minds. Therefore, we must try and understand the teachings of the great ones, not merely with our minds, but with the higher intellect and the heart.

Whatever happens; happens for the best; there is a reason for everything. God knows the best. He knows what is good for us. Hence we should surrender ourselves to God. At every step we must call out to Him and say, "Thy will, not my will, be done! Lord, do Thou protect me, take care of me!'

Is there anyone who has not gone through suffering? Is there anyone who has not faced any difficulties? Suffering and happiness are the two sides of the same coin. It is the dark nimbus clouds, which bring rain to the parched earth; it is the darkest hour of the night, which precedes the dawn. Therefore, we must learn to adopt a positive attitude to pain and suffering. If you are suffering now then your happiness cannot be far off.

Just as darkness teaches you to appreciate light, and intense thirst sensitises you to the value of water, in the same way suffering enables you to appreciate the experience of happiness.

If you are happy now, be sure suffering will soon follow. That is why, a wise man always remains composed in face of both sorrow and joy. A wise man does not feel unhappy in pain and suffering, he does not feel elated or excited when happy. He remains equanimous, in every circumstance, in any condition. He is ever thankful to God for whatever happens to him and around him. Because he knows whatever happens has a hidden meaning; whatever happens is for his good. Such a man is content; such a man is detached from the worldly affairs.

May I offer you a few practical suggestions to face pain and adversity in life?

1. We must take our mind away from the thought of suffering. If our attention is focused on suffering, it tends to get multiplied manifold.
2. In times of pain and suffering, we must learn to count our blessings. For those of us who are pessimistic to imagine that there are no blessings to count, there is a simple exercise. We can take a piece of paper and list all the things in our life which we have been blessed with.
3. We must learn to dissociate ourselves from the body, the mind and the ego. This is not easy, but it is the first step towards self-realisation. It is the mind that creates all our suffering; once we transcend the mind, there is no suffering at all – only peace and joy.
4. In all conditions and circumstances of life, we must continue to thank the Lord. We must make it a habit, to praise the Lord at every step, in every round of life. Even in the midst of fear and frustration, worry and anxiety, depression and disappointment, let the words, "Thank You

God! Thank You God! Thank You God!" be on our lips constantly. We will find that we are filled with a sense of peace.

5. Do not try to run away from trouble and pain. They are essential to our growth. God means us to face them with courage and acquire strength and wisdom.
6. Accept the Will of the Lord and fix your minds and hearts on God. Realise that God is always by our side, watching us, guiding us, guarding us and protecting us.

The best way to face the ups and downs of life is to accept them and cooperate with their inner purpose, all the while fixing our mind and heart on Him who has planned for each one of us the glorious liberty that belongs to children of the spirit.

Friends, we all know that life is not a bed of roses, but a battlefield, which requires all the strength of the spirit. The strength of the spirit is far more powerful, far more important, than the strength of the body. Therefore, our ancient rishis called it *atma-shakti*. Those who have this *atma-shakti*, are the ones who can face life with ease and grace, as the great saints have practically demonstrated to us.

We have heard it said in the Gita, that waters cannot wet, fire cannot burn, swords cannot cleave and wind cannot dry the immortal *atman*: here upon this earth, pain and suffering too, do not touch the realised soul. The secret of handling pain is to embrace pain, like a welcome friend!

My dear brothers and sisters, my last thought to you is – Do not search for happiness in material things, in pleasures in luxuries of life. True happiness comes with peace of mind, and peace of mind comes with contentment. He who is content is peaceful and he who is peaceful is happy. Worldly goods will never satisfy you, because the desire to have more will disturb your mind. In the *Yoga Vashista*, it is said that heaven has four guards. If you make fellowship even with one guard, he will open the door for you and let you in. One of the four guards is contentment or *santosha*. Therefore, let us remain content and be content with every situation, because God knows the best. Thank him under every circumstance, under every condition. Thank him when you are praised or criticised. Thank him for good health and for illness. Thank him for sorrow, suffering and pain. Thank him for all the good things of life you enjoy, for all the joy and happiness you receive.

Great is the tragedy of man. He spends his childhood in ignorance, his youth in fun and frolic, his old age in disease and decrepitude. Awake, O my soul, and clinging to the Lotus Feet of the Lord, cross over to the Other Shore!

Detachment is the Way

Early in the morning I heard a voice: I have been separated from you O Madhav, for many years. Let this life of mine be an offering unto you.

Fortunate is the one who hears this call. Fortunate is the one who awakes to the reality. My beloved, my Lord! I have lived many lives in separation from you. My beloved, I surrender; I offer my life at your lotus feet. *Bahut Janam Bhicharey The Madhav, Eho Janam Tumharey Lekhey!*

My dear brothers and sisters, everyone, every being, be it human beings, animals or insects, each and every creature craves for happiness. Every human being is in quest of happiness. In fact, the goal of every human being is to achieve happiness, to live a happy life.

What is happiness? What is true happiness?

Alas! Very few of us know the meaning of true happiness. The entire world is involved in a million hassled activities. Ask them, ask these people who are working from morning till night; ask them what they want to achieve. Many of them will say to you that they want success; because they feel success will give them true happiness. There are others who strive very hard to make money because they feel wealth and money will bring them happiness.

But can success, money, wealth and power bring us happiness?

A wise man tells us: "We come from God, who is Eternal Bliss. We will eventually return to Him who is Perfect Bliss. Between our coming here upon this earth and our return from hence, we undergo a lot of experiences that are mixed, with shades of joy and sorrow. It is these *experiences* that the soul craves, as an intermission between its dwelling in a state of bliss. Therefore, let us value and cherish these experiences. They help us evolve. They help us grow in maturity and wisdom."

When we put down everything to experience, when we accept everything that happens to us as Divine *prasadam* coming from the spotless hands of Him whose plans for us are perfect, we will cease to complain of sorrow, suffering and unhappiness. We will rejoice in the awareness that all is for the best in this best of all possible worlds!

Money, power, success, achievements and accomplishments – these are, for most of us, means to an end: and the end of human pursuit is happiness.

It must also be said, that from the ancient times, men have also sought to define the meaning and the 'art' of happiness. I would say thousands of books, articles and treatises have been written upon the subject. Poets, philosophers, teachers, scientists, psychologists and others have given us formulae for happiness. With all this wisdom available to us, are we really happy?

Leo Tolstoy begins his famous novel Anna Karenina with these unforgettable words: "All happy families are alike. But every unhappy family is unhappy in a different way."

That is indeed a perceptive remark: unhappiness has manifold causes and manifold manifestations! We are all unhappy for very different reasons.

Many young men and women who are single, are anxious to find the partners of their dreams, and think that they really cannot be happy, unless they are "settled" in life.

Young couples struggling to bring up children and coping with financial cares and anxiety for the future look back on their "days of freedom" as singles and sigh for the carefree days of the past that can never return.

Marriage, therefore, does not guarantee happiness!

Graduates fresh out of college and university, worry about their jobs, their 'placements' in suitable positions. If only they would be hired by a multinational or a big company, they think they would be delighted.

Many fresh recruits starting work are put off by their working conditions. They begin to feel they are underpaid and overworked; they feel they are not appreciated; they think others are paid more.

Employment does not guarantee happiness.

Politicians struggle to achieve positions of power in the state. Once they get into power, they find they have to struggle even harder to retain that power. The least indiscretion or mistake makes them fall out of favour with their party or the people, and they realise that being in power is not exactly a bed of roses. And should they be thrown out of their positions – they become the unhappiest of people, complaining, protesting, looking for supporters and clambering desperately to 'climb the greasy pole'.

Power, then cannot always bring us happiness.

We all want to be happy – but there are so few of us who are truly happy!

Man runs after happiness as camel runs after a mirage of water in a desert. Man runs after material things, outside of him. But my dear friends, happiness comes from within. It comes from oneself and one's relationship with others.

Have you heard of that rare breed of deer known as the musk deer? We are told that Musk deer is the fastest running animal. It carries the much sought after natural fragrance of musk deep within its system. When the deer gets the fragrance of musk, it runs hither and thither to get it. It runs far and wide, and yet it cannot find the musk, the source of the fragrance, which is within itself! Poor deluded creature, we say. But similar is our condition as human beings; we carry the seeds of our happiness within us. It is there, we are born to be happy; yet we run wild hankering after material goods.

The scriptures say, "This body is the shrine of God," these are profound words. The body enshrines the soul - the divine spark, the soul is ever peaceful! But our mind? When does it rest? It runs wild like an unbridled horse. Our senses? We yield to them, because we live on the surface.

A research worker who had the opportunity to live and work in various countries of the world, tells us that wherever she went, she made it a point to ask people if they were happy. She says that she had started off with the assumption that men and women in the 'richer' and 'more developed' countries would have fewer problems, and return more positive answers to her query. To her surprise, she found that this was not the case.

Some of the most 'developed' and 'advanced' countries in the world, with the highest per capita income, are facing peculiar problems. The burgeoning divorce rate and the break-up of the family are causing serious problems in countries like Sweden. The longevity of life, the increased life expectancy of retired people is posing a threat to the welfare system of countries like Germany and Switzerland; to put it bluntly, old people are living longer, but there are no young people willing to care for them at home.

You may be amazed to hear this – the only positive response to her question came in India. Yes, India, which the world regards as an undeveloped country, with all its poverty, its social problems, its teeming one billion plus population, its polluted rivers and its filthy cities – people here were happier than the affluent citizens of western countries! How was this possible?

It is not that there are no unhappy people in India. It is just that in their perception, they were happier than many others – people with higher standards of living, higher per capita incomes, bigger homes and better amenities!

Yes, people everywhere (including India) are unhappy. That is not surprising – what is surprising is, they do very little to change their condition, to make themselves happy. Instead, they only blame other people, outside causes and events for their unhappiness.

Bhutan was in the news in this regard. Do you know why?

It is because Bhutan has the highest gross national happiness. The King of Bhutan in 1972 coined the word gross national happiness – GNH in place of the economic concept of gross national income – thereby telling all the developing countries, that materialism and consumerism do not lead to man's happiness. Other inputs, other ingredients are required for happiness.

There is a book written by Dr. Rekha Shetty, with the title – *The Happiness Quotient.*

She has given conditions required for happiness.

1. *Dharmic* living
2. Family bonding
3. Social bonding
4. Good focused mind
5. Physical wellness
6. Work/job as an offering (to the Lord, to the society, to mankind)
7. Emotional well-being

I am glad, that at last man has begun to realise that material wealth cannot bring happiness. In fact, happiness does not come from outside, it comes from within.

A famous poet – a saint of Maharashtra sings:

> O man, you have roamed a great deal
> In the outer world.
> You have gone hither and thither.
> You have picked flowers, fruits and pursued innumerable activities.
> But all you have acquired is weariness.
> Now it is time to soar in the endless inner spaces of your being.
> What you are seeking can be found there
> In its fullness.

"As you watch it, your life turns to dust," sings Kabir. The world is transitory; everything we see around us is perishable. Not realising this, we try to build upon this bridge!

It was Bhartrihari who said:

> I thought I was enjoying sense pleasures;
> I did not realise *they* were enjoying me;
> I thought I was spending my time;
> I did not realise it was spending *me!*

We are all restless; we are dissatisfied; we are unhappy – and yet we refuse to change! We keep on doing the same things over and over again. Thus is our life spent, in futile effort and fruitless actions.

How many of us can honestly say we are happy? From all the available evidence, it would seem that true happiness is something of a rarity in the world today. In fact, many writers assert that unhappiness is the most prevalent feeling in the world now.

What are we going to do about it? How are we going to reclaim the happiness that is our birthright?

Attachment of any kind, as the Gita tells us, leads to suffering. *Raga, abhinivesha* (clinging and attachment) as it is called, is an impediment – not only on the path of liberation, but also in the attainment of personal happiness. On the other hand, detachment is one of life's greatest lessons for those who seek the true joy of life.

The tendency to accumulate material wealth, the craving for more and more, is the root cause of human unhappiness. Greed, one of the seven deadly sins, binds people with fetters that shackle their capacity for self-fulfillment and inner harmony.

Modern day best-selling author, Dr. Wayne Dyer, too, agrees with this truth. He tells us that it is just not possible to live one's life in joy and peace within the restricting structures of materialism, greed and accumulation.

"The perpetual pursuit of more and more," he tells us, "only begets loneliness and unhappiness."

Dr. Wayne Dyer lists the following as our "most common" attachments:

1) Attachment to material wealth and goods: The more we are attached to a house, a car, a piece of jewelry or an object, the more we lay ourselves open and vulnerable to unhappiness. The desire to possess leads gradually on to the impulse to accumulate and hoard.

   When you start accumulating material possessions, and start comparing yourself to others, your eyes, mind and heart are focused on things like wallets and bank balances. You fail to realise that inner fulfillment cannot be achieved from 'outer' things.

2) Attachment to other people: 'Possessiveness' in personal relationships acts like poison. When we try to monopolise the affections of our near and dear ones, when we try to run their lives according to our rules, we are striking at the very root of our personal relationships. Therefore, it is necessary to cultivate 'detachment' even towards the people we love.

Detachment does not mean indifference or lack of care and concern. It only means you stop attempting to control others, and avoid judging others on your own terms.

Here, as elsewhere, love is for giving – not for taking or demanding!

3) Attachment to the past: It does us no good to cling to the past, for the past is something to which we can never return in reality.

I read about a woman who fell on hard days when her husband died. Left to fend for herself and two children, she regressed into her past – her childhood in which she had lived a comfortable life as the adored daughter of well-to-do parents. She began to dress in the style of the 1930's, talk and behave in the manner of those days to such an extent that she became the butt of people's ridicule.

It is a serious mistake to become the slave of your own past.

4) Attachment to one's form and figure: Some people become obsessed about their physical appearance to such an extent, that they cause themselves great misery.

The Greek myths tell us of Narcissus, a handsome youth who was so carried away by his own good looks that he spent all his time in looking at his own reflection. Thus he broke the hearts of many young maids who loved him and longed to marry him. As a punishment for his self-centered, self-focused attitude, he was turned into a flower that grows on the banks of ponds and streams – bending over to look at its own reflection in the water.

Today, 'narcissism' is a term psychologists use to describe an unhealthy obsession with oneself and one's own appearance.

A great Indian yogi puts it thus:

The Saints tell us to treat this human body but as a temporary residence. Don't be attached to it or bound by it. Realise the infinite power of the immortal soul which dwells within this corpse of sensation.

5) Attachment to ideology: Some people are so passionate about their beliefs, their values and what they consider to be right and wrong, that they resent everyone who disagrees with them.

There are very many fanatics who consider their religion as the true religion, their God as the true God, and their scripture as the only true scripture.

They utter curses and damnation on all those who don't share their religion. This is of course, bigotry of the worst kind.

6) Attachment to winning: Everyone likes success – but success should not turn into an obsession.

Do you remember the wicked stepmother in the fairy tale, who uttered those unforgettable lines:

Mirror, mirror on the wall, who's the fairest of us all?

As long as she 'won' the contest, and the mirror replied, "You!" she was very happy. But the moment she ceased to be "the fairest", she turned ugly – metaphorically speaking!

When we are obsessed with the need to win, we become incapable of enjoying the great and priceless gift of life.

We must get out of this futile quest, this endless cycle of pursuing material pleasures and make our lives meaningful!

Detachment is the way!

Become aware of the value of the human birth. It is priceless. It has been bestowed upon each one of us for a specific purpose — that we may realise what we are, whence we came, and hither we are to return.

The Endless Quest

There is one question which we face in life repeatedly:

How can we get out of this futile quest, this endless cycle of pursuing material pleasures and make our lives meaningful?

They tell me that in American schools, the grades that students dread most are 'F' and 'I'. F stands for Failure; many of you might have guessed it; 'I' stands for Incomplete. They indicate 'underachievement' – not a good reference in professional circles!

When this happens to us in school or college, there are generally people around us to help us get out of the underachiever's syndrome. Teachers, friends, parents and guidance counsellors talk to us, motivate us and reassure us that we have the potential to perform better. But in the spiritual quest to fulfil the goal of life, we need the guidance and grace of a Guru, a spiritual mentor! If we do not 'improve our grades' we will turn out with "zero" grades when we face our Creator!

The great Nineteenth Century scientist Charles Darwin argued that life on earth began with very simple single celled organisms, and later developed into the many complex and varied life forms that we see around us today. He said that Natural Selection was one of the major mechanisms driving evolution. Thus Man evolved from primates and apes through a process of natural selection.

For Hinduism and many other Eastern Faiths, the issues and concerns raised by modern science are not important. For the true follower of the Hindu way of life, the focus is not on how life began, but on the *purpose* of life, which is to reach *moksha* (the ultimate freedom from reincarnation).

In one sense, according to Hindu philosophy, all species on earth including humans have not 'evolved' from lower forms; on the contrary, they have 'devolved' or come down from a high state of pure consciousness. For example, the scholar Michael Cremo proposes that human beings have not evolved from other animals, but they have *devolved* down from a spiritual world. This world is *Sat Desh*, (translated as "True Home"); it teaches us that a spiritual homeland exists eternally; it is the location where spirits dwell before they enter material bodies on earth.

According to the our ancient scriptures, the remedy to free oneself from the evil of devolution, is to cast off materialism, and realise one's true spiritual nature, which is that of *Sat Desh*, the homeland of spirits. A Hindu scholar describes *Sat Desh* as "The highest region, made purely of spirit substance and inhabited by pure spirits — pure because they are uncontaminated by matter or mind. There are countless spirits and they enjoy the greatest conceivable happiness".

I do not know what theory of creation you subscribe to: but let me say this; the purpose of this human birth is to attain Liberation or *mukti* from this endless cycle of materialism and worldly pleasures. If you believe that man came from a higher spiritual state to this 'devolved' state here upon earth, this human birth is still the easiest and quickest way for man to attain to his former, uncontaminated state of pure consciousness-bliss or *sat-chit-ananda*, as it is called. We are still the crown of God's creation, because this special route is open to us through our human birth!

This great gift of the human birth is bestowed on all of us – billions after billions of human beings, down the ages – but how many of us have realised its value?

Our scriptures tell us that there are thousands upon thousands of beings, including *devas*, demi-gods, insects, worms, flies, beasts and birds that God has created in this vast universe, one speck of which is this planet that we human beings call our home. There are in all, 8.4 billion life forms that a soul may enter at the end of any life cycle. In other words, each one of us has an approximate 0.00001% chance of receiving a human form again in our next lifetime!

Of all these creatures, it is only humans who are given the opportunity for Liberation from the circle of birth, death and rebirth. It is believed that one is born as a human being only when one has performed good *karma* in overwhelming measure in one's previous birth – in other words, one must have a credit balance of good *karma* to be blessed with this human birth.

This is why our saints and sages emphasise the inestimable, invaluable attainment that is human life. "You have been blessed with a human birth, which is difficult to attain," Adi Shankara tells us. "Don't waste the precious moments of your life in pursuit of sensual pleasures." Tulsidas too emphasises the same truth: "This human body is the gateway leading to liberation. Having attained it, you must strive to take care of your spiritual progress."

The question is: are we doing justice to this priceless gift that God has bestowed on us?

The scriptures say, "This body is the shrine of God"; these are profound words. The body enshrines the soul - the divine spark, the soul is ever peaceful! But what about our mind? It runs wild like an unbridled horse. What about our senses? We yield to them, because we live on the surface.

God gave us two eyes and two ears; but he gave us only one tongue. This is a clear indication that he meant us to talk less! Therefore we have the wise saying: speech is silver, silence golden. I would go one step further and say – silence is divine! In silence, you can hear the still, small, inner voice which can give you guidance from the inner power that resides within you.

God blessed us with two eyes – to behold His beauty in all that is! For is not this magnificent earth a grand testimony to His power and glory? So he gave us eyes, to see and enjoy the beauty of nature; to watch and experience the unfolding of night, dawn and the beautiful shades of twilight, to see the clouds burst, and rivers flowing, and the rhythmic tides of the sea rising and falling.

But what do most of us do with our eyes? We waste the great power of *chakshu* by watching mindless, distracting, misleading shows filled with *hinsa* and *kama* – violence and lust! By watching such shows repeatedly, we only allow these base emotions to be awakened within us.

Have you heard of the Northern Lights? It is the spectacular, natural display of sunlight in the northernmost regions of the earth, at a distance of three degrees to six degrees from the North Pole, caused by the energy charged particles which exist in that region. By all accounts, it is a magical, mystical experience to behold!

Let our eyes behold the beauty of the Beloved in all that we see. To behold the face of the Beloved in the radiance of a flower or in the fresh green of the grass and the leaves or in the magical serenity of moonlight is as rare and beautiful as the mystic Northern Lights!

God gave us two ears – not to listen to idle gossip and senseless rumours, but to hear His praise, to hear the resounding harmony of His Name Divine!

Through our nostrils, we breathe the breath of life. I cannot tell you how vital breath is to human life; not just in terms of oxygen to the lungs, but in its capacity to raise our consciousness to a higher level. Breath is the essence of life;

when it is purified, it opens the door to the inner life. Let us be conscious of the power, the value of every breath we take. Be conscious of your breath. Pause to take deep breaths whenever you can, during the day. As you breathe in, feel that your spirit is unfolding. As you breathe out tell yourself that you trust the world, that you trust life and that your faith in God will carry you through your darkest days.

Friends, with each breath, a precious moment passes by; we have spent one of our precious moments away; what have we done with that golden moment which will never ever be ours again?

Time is passing by! None of us can ever be sure how long we will be here in this human form. It may be that many years are left to us; or it may be that our days on earth are numbered. Whatever the time left with us, we have to make the most of it, put it to the best possible use. And this is certainly not to eat, drink and be merry, but to devote it to the Lord.

Let us ensure that our higher-self manifests itself in this human birth. Let our eternal bond with the Divine be strengthened here, during this lifetime.

> *Bahut Janam Bhicharey The Madhav,*
> *Eho Janam Tumharey Lekhey!*

Let my life be an offering unto Thee, O Lord!

Hinduism outlines four *purusharthas* or goals of life: *artha, kama, dharma* and *moksha* – or, to settle for a simple translation, wealth, desire, duty and liberation. And the best part of these goals is that you do not have to choose any one: you can legitimately choose and pursue all four, as you evolve spiritually. It may also happen that as you achieve each goal, your consciousness may rise until you decide that ultimately, there is only one goal that matters... the highest that we can aspire to!

The highest goal in Hindu thought is the goal of *moksha* or Liberation – freedom from worldly bonds, freedom from ignorance and illusion, freedom from the eternal cycle of birth-death-rebirth. The purpose of this human birth is to free ourselves from this vicious cycle. We may imagine that freedom is doing as we please; we may labour under the illusion that freedom is the ability to fulfill all our desires and satisfy all our sensual cravings: but we must understand that all this is only going to shackle us deeper and deeper in bondage. True freedom is the capacity to do what we ought to do, to follow the path of goodness, truth and *dharma*, to be able to live with a pure heart, a clear conscience and an untainted mind. Freedom is breaking away from bad habits, addictions and wrong attitudes; freedom is conquering the lower self; freedom is the ability to rise to the highest level of consciousness and the purest level of thought that we, as human beings, are capable of! It is this level, this height of awareness that we reach when we follow Sri Krishna's profoundly simple, yet powerful advice in the Gita: "Whatever you do, whatever you eat or pray, do it as an offering unto me!"

We need to introspect on our life, whenever we find ourselves drowning in mundane routines. We need to ask ourselves, "Why did God create me?" or "Why am I here?" or "What is the purpose of my life?"

I don't think a flippant answer to these questions will satisfy you. As Socrates put it with such clarity and certainty, "The unexamined life is not worth living."

Philosophers, theologians, scientists, and, indeed, thousands upon thousands of ordinary men and women have reflected upon these and other related questions such as, "What is the meaning of this existence?" "What is life all about?" and "Where is this life leading me?"

The meaning of life is deeply tied up with our views of religion, philosophy, the human condition, the pursuit of happiness and our concepts of morality, ethics, good and evil.

Nihilist philosophers deny all meaning to life. The individual's search for meaning, they claim, is in fundamental disharmony with the essential meaninglessness of life.

As for me, probably you know by now that that my views are inclined to the spiritual: I believe life to be God's greatest gift to us. And the best thing that we can do to fulfill the purpose of this life is to make of it an offering unto the Lord!

> *Bahut Janam Bhicharey The*
> *Madhav, Eho Janam Tumharey Lekhey!*

The saint who gave us this beautiful *bhajan* was none other than Sant Raidas. He was a wonderful member of the great *Bhakti* Movement in medieval India, which defied all boundaries and restrictions of caste and creed and status, to help the masses of this country reach out to the Lord in pure devotion, defying all mediators as well as all set dogmas and rituals. The singing saint Mira chose Raidas as her Guru. One of their deeply spiritual encounters is told to us as follows.

Mira Bai was once perplexed by a spiritual dilemma; she sought out her Guru and stood before him with folded hands. At that time, the cobbler saint was engaged in treating the leather with color, for making footwear.

Without looking up from his work, the saint asked, "Who is it?"

"It is I, Mira," the Rajput queen replied, in all humility.

"I...you... Mira...who? And if you are mine, then who am I?" said the saint, still not looking up at the visitor.

These words sent Mira into a deep inner quest. She bowed her head and stood still, in deep silence.

Still busy dipping leather in colour, still not looking up at her, he asked, "Why have you come to me?"

Mirabai replied: "*Prabhuji*, I have come in search of the truth."

Sant Raidas smiled. "A strange choice you have made! If you are in quest of truth, then why have you come to a cobbler? You should have sought out a great *jnani* like Tulsidas. He lives in Banaras, you know."

So saying, the saint glanced at his visitor, and exclaimed, "Oh! You have been splashed with my colour!"

While he was treating the leather with the color, drops of the tan color had splashed on Mirabai. Hearing these words, Mira's consciousness began to rise and she reached a state of *Samadhi*. She began to dance and sing in ecstasy, for she had attained self-realisation!

This is the kind of inner transformation that even a chance meeting with an enlightened soul can bring about in our lives!

I would like to end with the words of the beautiful *bhajan* '*Sukh Sagar Mein Aike, Mat Jao Pyasa Pyare*'. It is one of Gurudev Sadhu Vaswani's immortal compositions. It is a *bhajan* that stirs within us an urge for the higher ideals of life. The song awakens the slumbering spirit; a sudden realisation dawns upon us: my life is precious. Let me make the most of it. Let me not go back from this ocean of grace without tasting its sweet waters. Let me not go back exhausted. But let me drink the Divine Nectar and be blessed with bliss and peace!

Practise silence. Enter into the depths within you. In the depths within is the light that is wisdom.

The Inner Light

In every heart there is a point of light shining. It is the light divine. You can see it only when you turn within.

My beloved Master Gurudev Sadhu Vaswani has written a beautiful small book, titled, *'In the Veil of Dawn'.* This book is a gold mine of wisdom. It describes the light glowing in the interior of the heart.

Rishis of ancient India have described the human heart as a cave; deep inside is this light which shines bright. It is a point of light within. This light is beautiful to behold.

Man is ever in search of inner peace. He is in search of this light. He climbs mountains, he trudges over deserts, he travels to the poles to catch a glimpse of Northern or Southern Lights; but all that is in vain. What he needs to do is turn within. Enter the cave, the dark deep cave of your heart, and behold! The bright point of light, magical, eternal, and overwhelming, fills you with its radiance.

You may commit many sins; you may live a life which is evil and dehumanising. All that is outside the range of light. The dark evil doings are on the surface of life. All this evil can never, ever extinguish this light, for it is eternal. The day this light pierces the darkness of the heart and glows with its unique inner radiance, you will receive answers to your many questions. Once you have its vision, you will know your true identity. You will know the reason why you are here. You will know the purpose of your life. You will clearly see the goal and the path you must walk to attain it.

This physical body should be a temple of worship. For it enshrines the Light. That is why it is said, *Shariram Brahma Mandiram*: the body is the temple of God. We should enter this temple and have His *darshan*, rather than roam/wander far away in search of Him. Unless we witness this light within, we will not be able to experience God. The vision of this inner light is God realisation.

True, the light of the *Paramatman* shines within each one of us: but alas, we live in the outer darkness, unaware of the Light within. Like the aristocrats of the Medieval ages, we are absorbed in hunting – pleasure-hunting in the forests of the senses. What do we know of the indwelling Light?

Let me repeat, the Light inextinguishable dwells within each one of us, but we cannot see it, for it is hidden behind veils of ignorance, veils of mind and matter. The great wall of the ego stands between us and the *Paramatman* – and we cannot see the Light Divine. It is the Guru who can destroy the great wall of the ego, and lead us from darkness to light.

The 'Third Eye', the Inner Eye of the Spirit remains closed for most of us, its vision impaired by our bad *karma*. The cataract of the ego, the veils of arrogance and pride, have covered this inner eye completely. The Guru is the 'eye' specialist, who can restore our inner vision.

The Guru reaches out to us, and with his grace, annihilates the ego; he tears away the veils of ignorance which shield us from self-realisation; he reveals our true identity to us – *Tat Twamasi!* That Thou Art! It is his grace that liberates us from bondage to the circle of life and death. This gift of Grace has devolved on the Guru from God Himself – for God knows that the world is in dire need of Grace. His Presence is of course Universal: He gives us the Guru, for our individual benefit, for our personal liberation. This is why, our ancient scriptures enjoin us to venerate the Guru as God:

Gurur Brahma, Guru Vishnu
Guru Devo Maheshwara...

In this human birth, we cannot see God in person; but it is our good fortune that we can see the Guru, hear his *upadesh*, associate ourselves with daily *satsang*, accept his gracious *prasad* – indeed, grasp his holy feet firmly – and through Him, all God's blessings and all God's grace will come to us!

Once a very old man came to see me. He could hardly walk. He said to me, "I have come to seek your blessings. I am going to Haridwar, to see the Laxman Jhoola." I was concerned for him; I asked him, why he was so intent on taking up such an arduous journey at his advanced age. He replied, "It is my intense desire to see the Laxman Jhoola; it is my dearest wish to have a dip in the sacred Ganga at the point where Laxman crossed the holy river. I believe I will have a vision of God when I behold that sacred spot."

In vain I told him of the radiance within; that Ram, Sita and Laxman were seated within him. Instead of taking an arduous journey to Haridwar it would be better if he sat at home and undertook the *sadhana* to get a glimpse of light within, for then he would not only have '*Darshan*' but he could be with Ram, Sita and Laxman, who were all seated on the *jhoola* of his heart.

My dear ones, this body is the temple of God. We have to realise this light if we are to experience the Supreme, the Divine, the Eternal, that is within us.

In the Bhagavad Gita, Sri Krishna tells Arjuna, "O Arjuna, I reside in every heart." In each one of us is the Divine Spirit. Just imagine, the Almighty, the power Supreme dwells within us. Each one of us is a potent Krishna. Yet we live like weaklings. At the slightest difficulty, before the smallest obstacle, we retreat, we give way and break down. We succumb to pressures and problems, we get caught in a vicious circle of desires. It is sad, that despite the great '*Shakti*' of Krishna within us, we despair and fall into melancholy.

"Ye are gods," Jesus said to the Jews. "Your substance is that of God Himself," said the Sufi teacher. "Whoso knows himself has light," said Lao Tse, the Chinese seer.

We are so obsessed, overcome by the material world of *maya* that we fail to realise this Divinity within us. That is why our Rishis urge us to know ourselves well.

Gurudev Sadhu Vaswani, repeatedly urged us, 'Awaken the *shakti* within you.' He opened an *ashram* in Rajpur and named it The *Shakti Ashram*. He opened another *ashram* in South India and called it, *Para Shakti Ashram*. He urged the youth to be strong, to awaken the *shakti* within; to be brave and accept the challenges of life, to tap the 'power house' of infinite energy within them.

May I ask every one of you to treat your body with the sanctity and respect it deserves? You cannot keep it clean and pure just by taking a dip in the sacred rivers, for I speak of a deeper, inner cleanliness and purity. Keep this body clean and pure. This body is a temple. What makes a place a temple? Every temple, church or monastery has certain things in common: the bell which calls the devout to prayer; the light or *diya* which sheds its sacred light all around. Both of these things are to be found in the temple that is our body. There is a light within every heart – call it soul or *atman*. The second is the chiming of what our ancient rishis called the *anahad shabda* – the inner chiming of divine bells. Within every one of us is the sound eternal. We are unable to hear the sound even though it is vibrating within us. In fact this eternal, primordial sound is universal and vibrates all the time. It is with the rhythm of this *anahat nad* that the whole universe works. This sound eternal is Divine, subtle, throbbing in every living matter and organism.

"Inside this body the sound sings
Inside this body the Light Shines"

These two lines from an ancient song show us the way. The light is hidden deep within and the sound is subtle and fine tuned. To hear this divine voice we have to cultivate silence and meditate; we have to subdue our senses and sublimate our mind, to the extent we can. When we do this, the *kundalini* energy rises above the lower consciousness and opens the door of the temple, of the *sanctum sanctorum*, to give us the vision of the light.

Many of us, alas, are so preoccupied with our mundane, worldly concerns, that we think these are not meant for us. We are content to plug our ear phones into the physical ears and listen to film music. We have neither the inclination nor the time to think of the matters related to Higher life. The rational mind questions the existence of God and dismisses the very idea of the *atman* as unscientific. As long as life moves on smoothly and there are no hurdles of any kind, man does not feel the need for God. Only when troubles strike, man looks for comfort and support from 'above' from a super power that is beyond him. Even those who have faith in God, are often shaken up by a single tragedy or a few untoward incidents in life. They lose faith easily and question: where is He? Why is He so unkind to me? Why does He allow me to suffer thus? This is natural. Unless and until you have glimpsed the light within, you are bound to doubt the existence of God. Unless and until you have heard the sound eternal and experienced the Universal Light, you are going to be tormented by doubts about Him, His existence and His Supremacy.

Awaken the spiritual power within you! This is the true meaning of self-realisation!

Guru Nanak, the Spiritual Master and the Founder of Sikhism traveled far and wide to spread the message of Harmony and to enlighten people about the Light Divine. Many seekers followed him. Often he was asked the question: "Where is God? Can you show Him to us?" He would say, "God is here, God is there, God is everywhere."

"But we do not see God," people would protest.

Guru Nanak's answer to this was, "You cannot see God with these two physical eyes. To see God you must open the third eye. It is through the third eye, that you will be able to have the vision of the Supreme. Once the third eye is open, you can hear the sound eternal, and also have the glimpse of divine vision."

Once the third eye is open, you will transcend this world of *Maya;* you will surpass this world of the five senses and the three dimensions; you will see the glory of the world which is of the fifth dimension; that world is vast, it is greater, a hundred thousand times greater than the exterior world you see with the 'two eyes'. Let me say to you, once you enter the world of the fifth dimension, you will be dazzled by its infinity; you will forget the world you live in; it will lose its relevance to you, for you will be in a pure eternal world of the spirit.

The third eye is referred to as 'Shiva's eye' or *Shiv Shakti* in Hindu mythology. Once you acquire the inner sight or second vision you will be able to see the light which is the source of our being. We are floundering in the darkness, because we are unable to see beyond the gross physical existence.

Who is sightless? Who is visually challenged? All of us are, said Guru Nanak. For we do not have the inner sight/ second vision. We are unable to see and experience the vast, beautiful, heavenly world within us.

Is it easy to open the third eye? Is it easy to open the 'inner' second vision? For this you have to do *Sadhana,* you have to make effort, you have to take radiant action to help you to see the light, the light which we all are in need of. For that is the purpose, the goal, the reason why we are born.

It is because of this light enshrined within us, that I ask you, to treat the 'temple' of your body with reverence. Keep it pure and clean. Make it sacred. Worship not the gross physical, but the light it houses. The two are different; as different as a temple of bricks and stones is from the deity, idol, the cross or the light that it enshrines.

The body has ten doors. The nine doors open outwards but the tenth door opens inward. (The nine doors are two eyes +

two ears + two nostrils + two excretion outlets and one mouth). It is the tenth door which opens inward, which should be unlocked. How may we unlock it? It is tightly shut and firmly latched. It needs some higher power to open it. It needs the grace of God and the Guru.

Yes, you have to work for the grace of God. You have to Love Him, plead with Him, call out for Him for the Grace to be showered on you. With His grace you will behold the beautiful vision of the Light Eternal, a spark of which every one of us here on this earth carries.

A true Guru lives in the Light and the Light lives in him. His presence is radiant, and it illuminates your soul.

The *jignasus* of ancient India constantly prayed: *"Tamaso ma jyotir gamaya!"* (From darkness, lead me into the Light!) This light indeed is the light of the Spirit. The Guru can kindle this Light in the heart of the receptive disciple. Therefore, is the Guru revered as a "Light bringer".

Lead me out of darkness into Light!

For centuries this has been the deepest cry of some of greatest the souls of India.

Out of Darkness, O Lord! Lead me into Light!

This is the greatest blessing that the Guru can bestow on us. He leads us out of the darkness of *moha* and *maya* into the light of detachment and peace.

After this realisation, we enter the Realm of Light; we will reach our eternal home illuminated by the Radiance of that Light.